'Match of the Day, *and this enjoyable, revealing and affectionate book about it, are out of the top drawer.*'

– Alan Tyers, Daily Telegraph

'Witty and insightful'

– Steve Wilson

'A cracking read.'

'Bloody funny with outrageous but true stories.'

– Gary Lineker

'Fascinating insight into football on TV.'

– Henry Winter

'Highly entertaining'

– Guy Mowbray

'A great read for those who love the inner workings of TV.'

– Dan Walker

WHY ARE
WE ALWAYS
ON LAST?

Running Match of the Day and
Other Adventures in TV and Football

PAUL ARMSTRONG

First published by Pitch Publishing, 2019

Pitch Publishing
A2 Yeoman Gate
Yeoman Way
Worthing
Sussex
BN13 3QZ
www.pitchpublishing.co.uk
info@pitchpublishing.co.uk

A CIP catalogue record is available for this book
from the British Library.

ISBN 978-1-78531-438-4

Typesetting and origination by Pitch Publishing
Printed and bound in India by Replika Press Pvt. Ltd.

Contents

For Amanda from Stockton,
to whom I owe everything.
Including the title of this book.

Acknowledgements

To all at BBC Sport, past and present – broadcasters, producers, technicians and support staff alike – I'm forever in your debt for the decades of camaraderie, dedication and shared love of sport. Particular thanks to Gary Lineker for writing the foreword, and to Andrew Clement, Michael Cole, Lance Hardy, Peter Allden and Gary again for taking the time to corroborate (or correct) my sometimes hazy recollections. Thanks also to Tony Bate, Ian Finch, Mel Cregeen, Phil Sibson, Jim Cullen and Jo Tranmer for supplementing my limited photo archive; and to two wonderful causes – Comic Relief and the Macmillan Cancer charity – for graciously allowing me to use their professionally taken images. As a first-time author, I am especially grateful to Charlotte Atyeo for her advice, encouragement and support, and to Paul and Jane Camillin, and all at Pitch Publications, for transforming my ramblings into a proper grown-up book.

I'd also like to express my appreciation to all my friends and family for their support and understanding as I spent the sporting summers at events and worked weekends and late nights all year round. Especially to my wife Amanda for putting up with more of the same during the writing of this book, yet still finding time to dispense improvements in style and grammar. Finally, thanks to my Dad for first taking his six-year old son to Ayresome Park one crisp February afternoon in 1971, and to my Uncle Michael and the rest of the Chipchase clan for sharing the several highs and many lows ever since. UTB.

Foreword
by Gary Lineker

Match of the Day has been the one real constant in my life, well aside from, perhaps, the first half dozen or so years and a couple of sojourns to Barcelona and Japan where, for obvious reasons, I couldn't catch it (no dodgy streams in those days). I watched *MOTD* every week growing up, occasionally featured on the show during my playing career – missing an absolute sitter against Villa in my first ever appearance when playing for Leicester – and post-playing days I was a pundit for a couple of years before eventually hosting the Saturday night programme when Des Lynam left in 1999. I have been the frontman of BBC Sport's flagship show ever since, albeit with a temporary intermission when ITV stole it from underneath our noses for three years back in the early 2000s. It is the dream job, of course, for anyone who loves the game. It would, though, be far less enjoyable and immeasurably more difficult were it not for those folk that whisper, or on occasions shout, instructions in my ear (well, not literally in my ear, even though obviously there would be bags of room) from a gallery above the studio or from a van in a car park if we were on site at a live game.

One such figure was the editor of the show. This person, for 15 years or so, was our author, Paul Armstrong. This is the guy who carries the heavy burden of putting together an hour and a half of television live – yes, live – every Saturday night. This is the guy who has to decide how long the edit for each game will last. This is the guy who allocates the length of time of chat and analysis between the pundits and myself after every game. And this is the guy who decides the running order. This is the guy who puts your team on last.

It is a tremendously difficult job. It is also an enormously interesting job and from time to time an incredibly frustrating job.

Paul was one of the very best in the business. For a decade and a half we worked together. He was a generally pessimistic soul, constantly worried, wandering around the production office rubbing the top of his head. He cared deeply about football, he had a real understanding of the game (Alan Hansen may disagree) and knew its history like few others (Alan Hansen would agree). He also had a wonderful sense of humour, which is absolutely essential in this business, and an ability to laugh at himself, as will become clear when you read this book.

It is a fascinating and little understood business. This book will give you a genuine insight into how sport on television works and in particular how, after more than 50 years on our screens, *MOTD* is still the immensely popular programme it is to this day.

Prologue

Match of the Day studio. 22.45pm. Any given Saturday pre-2014

Alan Hansen (live on air): 'Tha's inexcusable. We've seen time and time again, you'll win nothing with defending like tha'.'

Gary Lineker (raised eyebrow to camera): 'Well, I thought it was a great striker's finish.'

Alan Shearer: 'So did I. Lighten up, Hansen.'

Gary Lineker: 'Next it's to Selhurst Park ... our man on the gantry, John Motson.'

Director/rally driver (on talkback): 'And run VT.'

VT (videotape) of Crystal Palace v West Ham edit goes to air.

Me (on talkback): 'Well done, guys. But we're a minute over now, so we'll need to lose the second run of analysis out of the Chelsea game.'

Alan Hansen: 'But that was going to be a classic! Have you got your sums wrong again, Armstrong?'

That was how my Saturday nights flew by for more than a decade. If everything was running smoothly, only the first few sentences would make it on to BBC One. A good editor is like a good referee: their day's gone well if no one's noticed them.

From the turn of the millennium until 2014, I edited the vast majority of episodes of *Match of the Day*. TV terminology can be confusing: I was the editor, a bit like the editor of a newspaper, in charge of content, the running order and the general tone, not the other kind of editor, a videotape editor, who actually cuts the pictures for each match edit. That requires a specific skill I never possessed, as does directing the matches or the live transmission of the show. Yes, it does always go out live, which is why it occasionally goes wrong or looks a bit rushed when your team, whom I'd inevitably placed last in the running order, was then analysed in 30 seconds flat. Now that I've left the BBC (ear problems and live broadcasting don't mix, so I took redundancy in 2016), I can only apologise for being biased against everyone and always putting every team on last. I did the job longer than anyone in the programme's history, and it only started to feature full edits of every top-flight game during my time in charge (and continues to do so under my excellent successor, Richard Hughes), so it was all my fault.

When asked what the editor of *Match of the Day* actually does, I generally trot out two answers. Firstly, you're really only the custodian of the show. When it started in August 1964, six weeks to the day before I was born, it literally was the pre-selected match of the day. Then it was two matches, then three and a round-up when the Premier League started. Now it's all six to eight games played on the average Saturday and however many on a Sunday, but evolution, rather than revolution, has always been the watchword. Like a Swiss army knife or the London Tube map, it's an easily understood design classic and you'd be foolhardy to tamper too much with it. Even a slight rearrangement of the theme tune for a couple of FA Cup rounds in the late 80s led to questions being asked in Parliament, and a hasty retreat back to the original.

Secondly, when describing the editor's role during the programme, the best analogy I can come up with is that the director is the rally driver steering the show, and the editor is the navigator alongside him or her hoping they're holding the map the right way up, trying to anticipate the twists and turns in the road. Having been in the production office all day watching all the matches with the presenter and pundits (the best part of the week, by far), then helped plot the analysis, and talked to the commentators and the producers editing each match, I was also the cartographer who'd drawn up the map, so had to shoulder responsibility if we ended up in a programme-makers' ditch. *Match of the Day Live* was similar in that it involved plotting the studio elements: pre-match was generally planned and structured, half-time and post-match were mostly reactive, based around analysis, interviews and montages. That could go spectacularly wrong if, say, Hansen failed to realise we were live on air at Molineux, or BBC One wanted to skip extra time and penalties at 3-3 in the Steven Gerrard FA Cup Final because they had to get to *Doctor Who*. More of that later.

Part of the job was to anticipate the various ways in which a programme could go wrong and have a plan up your sleeve if it did. Decades of watching Middlesbrough had prepared me well for this role of worrier-in-chief. Gary Lineker – with the optimism of a striker who made umpteen runs per game into the box hoping to score every time – was often amused by my philosophy of 'expect the worst, and you may just get a pleasant surprise'. Once, on a coach heading for a live FA Cup tie at the Riverside, he spotted a signpost just off the A66 and shouted, 'Great Burdon – hey, Armo, is that where you're from?'

As for the other question I am often asked, how I landed what sounds like a dream job, that's a more muddled story. There was no real method to it – as you'll see, it was a 'career' more in the sense that I careered around the BBC in general, then BBC Sport in particular, for over a decade making films, working with an extraordinary array of characters from Brian Clough to Paul Gascoigne, experiencing everything from high comedy to profound tragedy before somehow blundering into a live Television Centre gallery with a running order (my running order), an earpiece allowing me to chat with, and allegedly steer, a broadcasting legend in Des Lynam, and my heart in my mouth as BBC One handed over and the titles ran. 'Der-der-der-der ...'

'If this goes wrong,' I thought, 'it will be like Cloughie's immortal description of Larry Lloyd's disastrous England display in a 4-1 defeat to Wales: "Two caps in one day – your first and your f-ing last."'[1]

---

1   It was actually Lloyd's fourth cap, after a gap of eight years. Being pedantic is the editor's curse.

1.

Sportsnights, and days with David Coleman

Before I move on to my BBC baptism of fire with David Coleman and Esther Rantzen (not at the same time, that really would have finished me off), here's how I set off on an unlikely route to more than a quarter of a century at BBC Sport.

I was born, and spent my first 14 years, in Smoggieland: the unglamorous, and in football terms less deluded corner of the North East. Teesside was booming when I was born in 1964, but it didn't last long. When my Dad was moved south by the area's main employer ICI in 1979, the local economy was already on the slide. We had Captain Cook, and in the case of my hometown of Stockton-on-Tees, 1820s glory with the world's first passenger railway and the invention of the friction match by James Walker the chemist, but in the modern era we had chemical plants, steel and sport. I attended Ian Ramsey Comprehensive School which was founded in 1963, the year before I was born.

All the well-known alumni listed on Wikipedia played sport at the top level: Olympic athlete and 5 Live commentator Alison Curbishley; former flying Leicester Tigers winger Steve Hackney; and, among a number of professional footballers, the 'combative' Lee Cattermole of Boro and Sunderland fame – or infamy.

I was never in that sporting bracket – I was far too much of a lightweight fancy dan to 'Cattermole' anyone, for starters – but we did live the clichéd existence of playing football every break time and after school until it got dark, then cricket every day from May until September. I recently discovered that one of the more talented Stockton lads I kicked a ball around with went on to play and score in international football. Come on down Martin Todd of the Bahamas, Gold Cup qualifying, 1999. Along with playing briefly up front at college with an Irish sporting legend, Brendan Mullen (rugby union, bit crap at football, but very quick), my sporting cv is slowly coming together[2]. Thanks, Facebook.

And I watched everything and anything to do with sport on TV. To my eternal regret, I remember the 1970 Mexico World Cup opening ceremony ('why are we called Inglaterra, Dad?') but not the best-ever tournament that followed. By 1971, though, I was across it all. Charlie George lying on his back after his FA Cup Final winner, David Coleman telling us excitedly that Colchester were now 3-0 up in the fifth round of the cup against the mighty Leeds, Johan Cruyff's Ajax beating the exotically named Panathinaikos in a Wembley European Cup Final, the equally exotic Bishen Bedi tying Boycott and co. up in knots in that summer's Tests, Geoff Lewis and the great Mill Reef winning the Derby from Linden Tree and Irish Ball, Lee Trevino pipping Mr Lu of Taiwan ('where's Taiwan, Dad?') to the Open, Eddie Waring describing Sid Hines's 'early bath' in the Challenge Cup Final, David Bedford being outpaced by a Finn and an East German in an epic sprint finish in the European

---

2   My brother John has the best sporting claim to fame in the family. He played junior football in Kent alongside future England international John Salako. Then, as a decent spin bowler at Leeds University in the late 80s, he and his team-mates sniggered as their opponents, an Indian youth team, sent out a tiny figure in a sunhat to face them. They weren't laughing when he despatched their bowling all over West Yorkshire. John felt much better about it when Sachin Tendulkar toured England with the Test team the following summer.

Championship 10,000m. I sat glued to them all in that golden year of 1971. I don't even follow some of those sports now, but if it was on TV – and unless you were a bit naff and wanted to watch wrestling, the ITV Seven or cliff-diving from Acapulco – that pretty much always meant the BBC and *Grandstand*, and I was there.

And I was also beginning to discover the joys of spectating. Durham, then of the Minor Counties, often played cricket at Stockton, and Yorkshire played a match a season at Acklam Park, Middlesbrough. We had family outings to high-quality flat racing at York. And we had the mighty Boro. Middlesbrough FC had never won anything, unless you counted the Amateur Cup back in the 1890s. They were poised to win the league both seasons that the world wars broke out, according to the old-timers, and had been robbed countless times in FA Cup quarter-finals – but we'd spent about half our existence in the top flight and produced a string of great local players like Wilf Mannion and Brian Clough.

The first game I saw was a 5-0 win against Norwich in February 1971 (Downing, Hickton (2), McIlmoyle, Laidlaw) and with Stan Anderson later replaced by Jack Charlton in his first job in management, and Bobby Murdoch coming in to supplement Graeme Souness and David Armstrong in a phenomenal midfield, I didn't see a home defeat at Ayresome Park until QPR won there in 1976/77, by which time they were established in the top flight. We didn't go to every home game, by any means – my Dad and uncle wisely kept me away from likely 70s flared-trousered flashpoints when the Leeds or Manchester United hordes came to town – but I was left with a wildly exaggerated faith in my club's prowess, which sowed the seeds for many future disappointments. I also only discovered later that most of the rest of the country viewed Big Jack's team as a carbuncle on the backside of the beautiful game. Away from home in that era of two points for a win, our uncompromising defence of Craggs, Spraggon, Boam and Maddren (as the peerless Boro writer Harry Pearson once wrote, 'sounding like a collection of Anglo-Saxon farming implements') booted the rest of the country up in the air and ground out countless 0-0 draws to Cockney cries of 'Borrring, Borrring Barrah'. Good. It served the 'soft southern bastards' right.

Then suddenly, I was one of them. A soft southerner, that is. My Dad was relocated to ICI's London HQ. We moved down to Kent and I found myself starting my 'O' level studies at Judd School, Tonbridge, a state grammar with an excellent academic record – some outstanding sixth-form politics and English teachers eventually helped get me good enough 'A' level grades to get into Oxford – but one which at the time was, socially at least, a desperate public-school wannabe. 'All fur coat and no knickers', as northern ladies of a certain vintage used to say about upwardly mobile women. Starting the fourth year there felt like arriving in outer space. There were no girls (a bit of a downer for a hormonal teenager who'd begun to enjoy their company); incomprehensible traditional maths (I'd been learning some trendy modern version); you were addressed by your surname and supposed to say 'Sir' back and, most appalling of all, there was no football. Until the summer term, when you could play cricket or tennis, there was only rugby (rugby union, not that other northern abomination), or if you were a lily-livered wimp who valued his teeth, you could go on an invigorating cross-country run instead. Those were your only choices.

In my first games lesson in Kent, I was asked what position I played. I explained that I'd always played football. 'You mean soccer,' sneered the games teacher, before shooting me a look so cold I was tempted to go back and fetch my coat from the changing room. He spent the next four years telling me to fasten my top button whenever he passed me in the corridor. The first XV thought he was great; he called them by their Christian names and took them on tours to places like Canada and Japan. The irony is that the top public schools like Eton, Harrow and Charterhouse had codified the rules of football, dominated the early FA Cup and still happily play the game to this day. Somewhere along the line, a confused young chap in a Warwickshire backwater had cheated by picking up the ball and, boy, were we going to suffer for it. Such was the snobbery about football, we weren't even allowed to play at break times. I was never going to overtake those who were steeped in chasing the egg and make the first XV, nor would I have wanted to, but I was able to kick and catch the non-sphere after a fashion, so managed to survive games lessons. I didn't play competitive football again – though I could soon do 1,000 keepy-ups on my own in the garden – until I reached university, by which time I'd lost out on the crucial years when you learn positional play and how to function as part of a team. And while I was quite bitter about it all at the time (no, really), looking back it did me a huge favour.

I made lasting friendships through the secret fellowship of football. Our neighbour in Kent was a warm, unstuffy Scottish chap called Doug McAllister. He and some friends had season tickets at Crystal Palace, so I often went with them to Selhurst Park when a seat was available, and at school, after a bit of digging around, I discovered some other undercover football heretics. John Luke had come to Kent from the Midlands and was a Villa fan – I'd always liked the Andy Gray and Brian Little-inspired team of that era – so we went to watch them whenever they came to London; Jon Rycroft's dad was from Carlisle, where the already-brilliant Peter Beardsley was coming through the ranks, so we cheered them on at places like Gillingham and Millwall (albeit very quietly when they won at the latter); Mark Turner and I went to as many Spurs games as we could, particularly during their Hoddle-inspired cup runs; and Chris Wise was an Arsenal regular and the only person I ever knew who was allowed to pay 90p to enter the quaintly named Schoolboys' Enclosure at Highbury while sporting a luxuriant moustache.

My close friend and talented musician David Eastwood, who sadly died much too young from a brain tumour, would happily go and watch absolutely any game of football anywhere, no matter how unprepossessing, so we watched Boro whenever they came to the south-east and always found a fixture somewhere in London every Saturday and most midweeks. David hated rugby. I have an abiding memory of him standing on the wing in the freezing cold, sleeves over his hands Denis Law-style, as I chucked the ball down the line from fly-half. He yelled, 'Oh no, I might get the ball!' and was promptly ordered to run a couple of laps of the pitch for his insubordination. One games lesson, when rugby was completely frozen off, we went to the gym for a makeshift basketball session. I was appointed one of the captains and decided to break with humiliating convention and pick my least athletic mates David and Jon first. I was duly given a detention by that day's games teacher, who happened to be a humourless former England rugby international, all of which just about sums the place up. I'm sure it's better these days – it must have entered at least the 20th century by now.

However, as the Americans discovered during Prohibition, if you drive something underground it tends to flourish and take on a whole new romantic allure. Football became something of an obsession, even as it increasingly became a pariah sport for the government and much of the wider country, while Boro went into a dismal decline which included two relegations before Steve Gibson and his consortium saved them from liquidation in 1986. The game had become a major part of my identity – I played two or three times a week (to a distinctly moderate standard) at university and still watched as many games as possible, in the flesh or on TV – so by the time I applied to become a BBC production trainee in 1987, football was central to my application process. A bit unorthodox, since I'd done a politics and philosophy-based degree; however, I was applying for a scheme which allowed you to spend two years moving around different departments, so I thought I'd probably end up in BBC News and Current Affairs, with its greater output and staffing levels, but at least have a stint at BBC Sport before settling down.

Part of the application process was to review a BBC show you'd watched recently. I suspect most of the other production trainee applicants opted for highbrow *Panorama* or a gritty drama, but instead I just let rip about an utterly boring, predictable *Match of the Day Live* Liverpool win (at Watford, I think) in which the whole production seemed to consist of one long drool about the men in red. Liverpool were the best team in the country for most of the late 70s and 80s, but they seemed to feature in almost every BBC live game. Norwich City even had an early fanzine in those days called *Liverpool Are On The Telly Again*. It seemed out of all proportion to their entertainment value for the neutral. Ian Rush would score on the break away from home against hapless team X, Hansen and Lawrenson would keep the ball between them and pass it back to Grobbelaar (as they could then) for the rest of the game and it would finish 0-1. Every live TV game for about eight years, or so it seemed. On this occasion, Rush wasn't even named in commentary by Barry Davies, but simply called 'you know who' when he inevitably scored on the break. 'Yes, I do bloody know who,' I think I wrote, 'he's live on my telly almost every sodding week.' Actually, I may have been more wry and subtle than that, but when I turned up for the selection process, at least the distinguished programme-making interview panel knew who I was. The 'token bolshie pleb' I suspect it said in their briefing notes.

Compared to today's graduate aspiring to a career in the media, my cv was bordering on the pathetic. I'd played sport at a modest level, and edited the college magazine briefly, but I was glad no one asked me to show them a copy. I suspect they'd have taken a dim view of the scurrilous, badly produced sub-*Private Eye* in-jokes, cartoons and gossip rag that it was. Actually, that's a bit harsh on the cartoonist – a first-year student called Richard Jolley passed on a whole supplement's worth of talent and satire a few weeks after arriving. These days, he's 'RGJ' in *Private Eye*. Even so, a typical 21st-century media applicant has spent three years on a dedicated media course, run the student radio station, launched their own YouTube channel, blogged about travelling the world, written an opera and had a couple of novels published, but fortunately those were more half-arsed times, and an unorthodox application in which I opted to review *Match of the Day* somehow got me on to their highbrow shortlist as the wild card.

I already had a place on a more traditional trainee print journalism course lined up. My Auntie Dorothy had written for the *Northern Echo* and once interviewed the Beatles when they played the Globe Theatre in Stockton. In my shambolic, unfocused way, I thought maybe I could follow in her footsteps. So when, to my great surprise, the BBC summoned me for an interview, I was quite relaxed about it. The waiting room was full of nervous wrecks whose parents expected them to be running *Newsnight* or BBC Drama one day, so I was at a considerable advantage with no one, including me, expecting anything to come of it. At that time, as a lazy student with only four channels available on the black-and-white portable in my room, I was up on pretty much everything TV-related. I just chatted about that for an hour and answered a general knowledge quiz heavily skewed towards popular culture. If I went through the same process now, I'd fail horribly. These days I can't keep track of it all, and only really watch sport and news live, record *Have I Got News For You*, *University Challenge* and *Only Connect*, and occasionally discover a good comedy series about three years after everyone else.

So, somewhat stunned, I signed the BBC's contract, put the print journalism career on hold, and turned up at Elstree for a six-week induction course in the autumn of 1987. I had absolutely no idea how TV was put together – some of BBC Sport's techies would say I still don't – so taking turns to direct, go out with a film crew and run cameras and sound equipment ourselves was just fantastic. Then it was time to start our attachments – three months or so working in different departments which, in theory, would end with us applying for a permanent job in an area to which we were best suited. I grew up enormously in those initial couple of years, and went from absolute beginner to fledgling producer, under the tutelage and withering gaze of Coleman, Rantzen and others.

But first came Mike Neville. Most people reading this will have no idea who Mike Neville is. Some keen students of TV may remember his regular accomplished contributions to BBC One's 1970s magazine show *Nationwide*. But if you're above a certain age and come from an area roughly between the Scottish border and the North Yorkshire Moors, the chances are you're well aware that he was one of the greatest broadcasters ever to draw breath. The greatest, if you listened to my elderly relatives who recounted with pride how 'that lot in London' wanted him to be a national star, but he'd chosen to stay amongst his own people. I later had it confirmed that this was more or less true and that Mike had effectively been TV's answer to Matt Le Tissier, choosing to spend his whole football career at Southampton. Better to remain a big fish in a small pond, loved beyond measure and never having to buy a drink in one part of the country, than to become just one more star amongst many – or worse, lose your identity altogether – on a larger stage.

Mike, an actor by training with a glorious speaking voice which became more obviously Geordie after a couple of drinks, had started at Tyne-Tees in regional TV's infancy before moving to anchor the BBC's *Look North* regional news show in 1964. He was a constant backdrop to my life until we moved south in 1979, a gentle but superb interviewer, dry and funny like a proto-Des Lynam, and, when required, an utterly brilliant improviser. I distinctly remember watching a *Look North* in the mid-70s when the technology crashed. Having tried – and failed – to link to every remaining item on the running order, Mike just laughed and picked up a copy of the *Evening Chronicle*. He put his feet on the desk and disappeared behind it, occasionally peeking out with observations like 'those Swan Hunter talks are going on a bit, aren't they?' or 'good result for Sunderland, eh?' until the problem was fixed. That's how I'd like to cope with a crisis when I grow up, I thought, lost in admiration.

For my first experience in real broadcasting to involve working with Mike on *Look North* was a thrill, equalled only by eventually taking charge of *Match of the Day*. I was only sorry that only one of my grandparents, my grandma Alice in Bishop Auckland, was still around to see it happen. County Durham folk singer Jez Lowe once recorded a song called 'Mike Neville said it (so it must be true)' and that was no exaggeration as far as my family, our friends and indeed a whole region were concerned. Forget Des Lynam leaving for ITV, or the *Great British Bake Off* going to Channel 4, Sol Campbell exchanging Spurs for Arsenal or Luis Figo moving from Barca to Real, when Mike left the BBC and *Look North* to return to Tyne-Tees in 1998, for an area with a strong sense of identity, this was a 'Snatch of the Day' to dwarf them all. When Mike died, aged 80, in 2017, the whole region – Tyneside, Wearside, Teesside and all the rest – put their usual petty divisions aside and mourned as one.

Back in 1987, Mike was unfailingly kind to me and his *Look North* show was the perfect place to embark on a TV career. The veteran Scottish news editor Ronnie Burns was terrifying but darkly funny, his team was mostly lovely and encouraging, and I was quickly allowed to make features on everything from DJ mixing at the legendary Mall nightclub in Stockton to poetry readings on the Shields ferry. Steve Sutton, the genial sports reporter who wasn't a lot older than me, was happy for me to tag along to any football – in fact on my second day there, he phoned Boro and told them to leave a press box pass for me on the gate at Ayresome Park for a game against Ipswich that evening. This was a privilege and a thrill, not least because the home team won 3-1 (Kernaghan, Pallister, Slaven), and it remained so throughout my career. My spell in Newcastle coincided with the first half of the 1987/88 season in which Bruce Rioch's post-bankruptcy Boro team of Bernie Slaven plus ten bleached blond local kids (including future England players Gary Pallister, Colin Cooper and Stuart Ripley), newly promoted from the old Division Three, duly raced to the top of their new league. When Boro were away from home, the young Paul Gascoigne at Newcastle and free-scoring Marco Gabbiadini at Sunderland were also providing plenty of excitement, and Steve and I would also go to Hartlepool and Darlington for FA Cup ties. It became my pleasurable task to cut the weekend's goals and quotes from the region together every Monday for the sports segment of the show.

Such was the approach to mucking in, and sharing the workload around, the team were more than happy to let me loose with opportunities I would never have had in the glare of network TV, and for that I will always be grateful. I was allowed to vision mix, that is, cut the live cameras, graphics and videotape to air, for the main evening half-hour show. Having not messed that up, I was soon studio directing on my own for the lunchtime and teatime bulletins. A less accomplished, or more insecure, presenter than Mike Neville could have kicked up a fuss or at least raised an eyebrow at some young pup being left in charge of proceedings, but Mike just quietly told me, 'It'll be fine,' and off we went.

Regional TV slots, then as now, involved 'opting out' of BBC One or Two. It may be a slightly different process in these days of BBC North East and Cumbria and co each having their own allotted digital channel, but back then I physically had to press a button in Newcastle, when London told us to 'opt, regions', in order to send our output to the transmitters in our region. I then had to press another button at an exact pre-ordained time at the end to switch the North East back to national programmes. This was exciting and a useful early taste of trying to make *Match of the Day* fit its slot, but it also presented a logistical challenge. Working on the established principle of 'three words a second' for script, and adding in the durations of the videotape clips, the show should be somewhere close to its allotted four and a half minutes. Even so, how could I ensure we'd be bang on duration and therefore opting back at exactly the right moment?

I needn't have worried. I soon discovered that Mike would calmly ask while we were on the last videotape clip, 'How long for the weather, Paul?' We'd have a Met Office summary written down and intended to fill about 30 seconds, but if it ended up needing to be nearer a minute, Mike would just improvise something about it looking like a good afternoon for a walk round the ramparts at Alnwick Castle, but you might want to think about eating your fish and chips indoors if you were heading down to Whitby. If, as happened at least once, my sums were out in the other direction and we only had five seconds to get off the air, he'd say something like, 'And the weather: min temp 10, max temp 12. See you later for *Look North*.' Five seconds, fifteen words. I'd cut back off the weather graphic at Little Richard piano speed to Mike in vision after the word '12', then back to the network after '*Look North*'. We'd then meet in the studio corridor. No debrief was needed, he'd just smile and pat me paternally on the shoulder. Mike Neville: a true broadcasting legend.

Towards the end of 1987, shortly before I moved on, I was asked to work on the North East element of *Children in Need*. Naturally, Mike presented this too, and I was roped in to help out as a researcher/floor assistant looking after the guests and getting them in and out of the studio during the local opt-outs from the national broadcast. In the middle of the evening, I was told Paul Gascoigne was at the stage door. My first thought was that Gazza wasn't in the running order, but it turned out this was an impromptu visit. I'd seen him play and knew he was going to be a bit special in that regard, but this was my first introduction to the (then 20-year-old) man. He was on the doorstep on his own in his Newcastle United tracksuit, said he'd been at the ground about a mile away, saw the show was on and, even though he had a game the next day, had decided to do his bit for 'the bairns'. He'd got hold of a bucket and walked down to Broadcasting House on Bridge Street, stopping off in every pub en route to persuade the Friday night punters to donate. His bucket was stuffed full of notes and coins – he politely declined my offer to come in and join the show on air, handed over the bucket, shook my hand and wandered off into the freezing cold Tyneside night.

So that was regional TV. The next leg of my apprenticeship came at the hands of arguably the most influential British sports broadcaster of all time. He was the soundtrack to most of my early memories of the biggest sports events on the planet. Whether it was 'Porterfield, one-nil' or simply a pause then 'the Olympic one hundred metres final', even as a small child I knew it was David Coleman growling at me, and it was time to pay attention. I can remember the hostage crisis at the Munich Olympics vividly, but it was only years later when I watched the live coverage back for the documentary we made for the centenary of the modern Olympics that I fully understood just how great a broadcaster he was: hour after hour of live, unscripted broadcasting, which had moved far away from sport into the realms of major international news, and indeed history. He was calm, concise, authoritative and unsensational in the most difficult of circumstances. David was a northern grammar school boy who, along with the pugnacious production pioneer Bryan Cowgill, had been in the vanguard of transforming the gentleman amateur's world of the early years of sport on TV into the professional, hard-nosed journalistic world I joined. He'd reported, commentated, presented and often apparently more or less produced and directed across all the flagship shows to an absurdly high standard for more than three decades. I was sent to BBC Manchester to learn what I could from him.

Even though my broadcasting career was just a few months old, I knew he was the daddy of them all, and the little I'd gleaned of his reputation suggested that he was demanding, and rather fearsome. So, it was with some trepidation that I went with the producer of *A Question of Sport*, Mike Adley, to meet David in the bar of the Midland Hotel in Manchester in January 1988. It was a Saturday evening, two Q *of* S shows would be recorded at the Oxford Road studios next day, and this was where the great man liked to hold court. 'David, this is Paul. He's joining us for this series from the production trainee scheme,' Mike said. David shook my hand, very firmly, looked me up and down and growled, 'Well, he'll know nothing then.' Mike Neville he wasn't, clearly. I just smiled and ploughed on, talking about sport and as little as possible about television for the rest of the evening. At least I knew about sport, and the fact that my head wasn't bitten off again as we all had a few drinks suggested that much had registered.

I soon learnt that it was all part of the Coleman method of testing you, and that bluntness and mickey-taking – it was too fierce for the modern catch-all term 'banter' – was just what he did. Once you were in, you were in. His team at *A Question of Sport*, or on the athletics circuit – and presumably in previous years on *Grandstand*, *Match of the Day* and *Sportsnight* – were galvanised by his very presence. I was reliably informed by the excellent, ultra-friendly production team – two of whom, Ray Stubbs and Ken Burton, I subsequently worked with for most of my career – that David, who by now was in his 60s, had mellowed almost entirely and was now something of a pussycat. Even so, it was pretty frightening that first programme Sunday to hear a growl of, 'Who wrote this question?' and be summoned on to the set and given the third degree about some half-baked swimming statistic I'd lifted from a reference book during the week.

Each show was rehearsed in the morning with two full teams of sports quizzers. This was partly to allow the cameras and lighting team a run through, but also so that David could test out whether the questions worked. Or, more to the point, whether he thought they did. Woe betide you if one of the quizzers raised an eyebrow at an answer. Up you'd go, blinking into the studio lights, clutching your research. 'Are you sure about this?' he'd growl. I was sent off on one occasion to phone Stan Greenberg, the BBC's athletics statistician, after David decided some fact or other I'd gleaned from our office bookshelf (no internet then) was of questionable provenance. But, for a wet-behind-the-ears, slightly sloppy ex-student, this was exactly the sort of rigour I needed. We wrote the questions, prepared biographies of all the guests, having phoned them for a chat, and had a lot of fun. Between rehearsals and the actual recording of the shows in the afternoon, everyone – David, resident captains Emlyn Hughes and Bill Beaumont, guests and families, production team – sat down to Sunday lunch. I don't know how or when this had evolved, but it was an inspired idea. David hosted, everyone relaxed and felt part of a team and for a guy like me who'd been playing a mediocre standard of university football less than a year earlier, it was a huge thrill to mingle with the leading sportspeople of the time. And although there was some tension behind the scenes when the shows were recorded, the fact that they weren't live and I wasn't in the hot seat made me mostly just pinch myself that I was doing this for a living.

For a fundamentally serious man, David took great delight in the occasional silly question. Ken was virtually given a lap of honour by him one week for a trick question featuring a ridiculous racing pigeon name. The first week I was there I came up with a riddle along the lines of 'what gradually moved 74cm in 56 years, but has gone nowhere since 1968?' The answer was Bob Beamon's long-jump world record. David liked it and used it, and I was inching, or centimetring, my way in. We also had that 'fill in the name' game featuring sportspeople who share names with Welsh towns and so on – Joanne Conway, Phil Newport and Ron Barry, since you ask – and because I was prepared to put in the hours to establish myself, I came up with quite a few of those. It also led to some silliness in the office which never made the air, such as the birth cycle 'missing names' round – David Seaman, John Emburey-o, and Foetus Gerulaitis, for the record.

The most creative element of the show for the production team was the mystery personality films – they actually were still films, not video – of sportspeople undertaking some activity or other, cut to music and generally entrusted to Ray Stubbs, who, before he moved to a front-of-camera role, was an imaginative producer. As part of my training, I was often sent to keep him company – we had a chaotic morning at Alex Higgins's country pile in Cheshire, and an afternoon in Southport with my later nemesis Alan Hansen. Alan got a bit cold during endless takes with the binmen and lorry Stubbsy had rustled up from somewhere, and because I happened also to be wearing jeans and the same brand of Puma trainers, I doubled for the Hansen legs and feet in a couple of shots. I probably should have declared that to a BBC Safeguarding Trust enquiry a long time ago. I can only apologise now to Bill Beaumont who was misled by my slightly shorter legs and said it was the jockey Walter Swinburne, who didn't look like me or Hansen.

But the most memorable of all – him again – was Paul Gascoigne. Stubbsy had mentioned in the office that instead of just cutting shots together to music, he wanted to make a film where the music was more central by asking a sports person to mime along with a musical instrument. It so happened that in February 1988 the *Daily Mirror's* Monty Fresco captured those famous images of Wimbledon's Vinnie Jones squeezing the poor lad's testicles during a game at Plough Lane. I came in on the Monday with the idea of getting Gazza to mime along on the piano to Jerry Lee Lewis's 'Great Balls of Fire'. A slightly risqué play on words, but not blatant enough to offend anyone, and a great piece of music into the bargain.

Stubbsy booked a music venue in Newcastle, hired a 50s teddy boy outfit and off we went. We thought it should work as an idea, but what we weren't prepared for was the gusto Gazza put into it. Before we knew it, he'd put on the costume and was vaulting the piano in his crepe shoes and running his hands up and down the keys. Glissando is the correct musical term, I believe, but I'm not sure even Jerry Lee ended up with bleeding hands from the sheer exuberance of his performance. Gazza just laughed and kept going. I know he's had a chequered life and done some stupid, self-destructive things, but some of the most sensible, undemonstrative football people I've known – Messrs Lineker, Shearer and Venables – love him beyond measure, and after those two encounters with the young Gazza it's easy to see why. That's before you even mention his phenomenal footballing talent. The mystery personality piece Ray eventually cut was fantastic and was given an unprecedented spontaneous ovation by the studio audience, some achievement for a minute-long pre-filmed segment.

As for David Coleman, he was not the sort of man who would ever want you to call him a mentor or even a major influence on your career, but he really was, and to many other people – Sue Barker and Steve Cram, to name but two current fine BBC Sport figures – over the decades. When he died in 2013, aged 87, Brendan Foster described David as the 'greatest sports broadcaster that ever lived'. While that may well be true, David would probably have dismissed such a suggestion as 'bollocks'. In his later years, he turned down the idea of a whole evening on BBC Two being given over to the vast collection of Coleman highlights from the archives with the words, 'Not even Barbara [his wife] wants to spend "*An Evening with David Coleman*",' and he didn't appear in the fine BBC Sport documentary that was shown for his 85th birthday and featured his family and some extraordinary footage of his unparalleled career.

I worked from time to time with David in later years on athletics – once displeasing him with a note I put in front of him as he commentated live on a London Marathon recap I'd edited, to the extent that he crumpled it into a ball and bounced it off the middle of my forehead while calmly listing several Kenyan athletes for the BBC One audience. I'd bump into him at an airport or hotel and he'd cheerily greet me with something like, 'What the hell are you doing here? Have you learnt anything yet?' and somehow, it would feel like a compliment. 'Quite remarkable', as he would claim he never said if anyone was feeling brave and mentioned *Spitting Image* in his presence: 'That was Ron Pickering, sunshine.'

Three months later, during which I discovered I was entirely unsuited to Schools Television, I embarked on what was to be my last stint for a quarter of a century or so working anywhere other than BBC Sport. In its own way, working with Esther Rantzen cemented my awareness that I was not a natural habitué of most of television, but it was a heck of an experience and learning curve. My arrival in the department then called Topical Features coincided with the build-up to the launch of a major new Saturday night Esther vehicle called *Hearts of Gold*, featuring the same production team that had recently finished making the latest series of her long-running Sunday evening fixture *That's Life*.

I went to their office in the famous and by-then dilapidated Lime Grove building to meet a couple of the bigwigs and was asked as an ice-breaker whether I liked *That's Life*. I almost laughed – well, of course I didn't. I was 23, a bit cynical, in recent years Sunday evenings had generally meant a homework or essay crisis rather than watching TV, and anyway the show was something of a byword for naffness. A bizarre mishmash of consumer stories and lighter pieces about talking pets and phallic-shaped vegetables was how I saw it. Have a look on YouTube if you think that can't be right. I mumbled something about not having watched it for some time, and they said this was going to be a different sort of series in any case, and I'd be useful if I knew more than most of them did about sport and popular culture, so I was in. The fact that I was paid my trainee wage from a central fund and would therefore cost their department nothing was probably a clincher, too.

They then outlined the premise behind the show – I sniggered inwardly – which was to film unsung heroes and heroines, lure them into a live studio under a pretext then surprise them with a tribute film, a Heart of Gold award and some kind of reward, an event or moment the research suggested they'd love. I could feel the urge to barf but decided to nod along instead. I was actually intrigued – these were really bright people (even if they were involved in a genre I didn't watch). I'd noticed a disproportionate number of glamorous women as I'd walked through the office, and I reasoned, rightly, that I might never work anywhere like this again, so I'd give it a go. What followed was one of the most full-on periods of my entire life. In her own way, Esther was like Coleman, but even more so. Despite being the queen of popular TV, she was phenomenally, forensically bright, incredibly demanding and involved in every single aspect of the programme making. She'd examine your research at every stage, and was present as every single item was edited, then scripted everything herself at an old-fashioned typewriter. The intensity of the work schedule was as extreme as the Olympics or World Cups I later worked on but was at that pitch for months on end. When I finally crawled out of there at Christmas 1988 at the end of their first series, I was looking forward to joining BBC Sport in the new year for a rest.

I arrived a month before the studio pilot show was to be recorded. Just a week after the pilot, a full series of eight programmes were scheduled to begin their Saturday evening transmissions. They'd all been tied up with *That's Life*, so very little was in place – I was sent out to vet possible stories, most of which had come from viewers' letters in response to an appeal in the *Radio Times*. Some were absolute red herrings, others were clearly never going to work in TV terms, but a lot of them ended up being made. And at every stage, Esther wanted to know exactly what you were up to, and why you'd formed whatever opinion you had. When I didn't have an opinion, I had to invent one and learn to defend it in programme meetings. The hours were insane, the pressure of moulding a BBC One peak time format on the fly was considerable, but the socialising was like being back at university. Far too little sleep, food and booze on the run, juggling relationships and office politics: it was the full madness of the media world as you see it in films and TV drama. The thought of living like that now gives me cold shivers, but in my mid-20s it was a blast.

A few of my career highlights still come from that time – a day with Bobby and Jack's mum Cissie Charlton in Ashington as she took the local infants' school football lessons, and a wonderful day's filming on the Isle of Wight with the late Stephen Lewis, who'd played Inspector Blakey in the 70s comedy *On the Buses*. The slightly strange, but nevertheless inspired, notion of director Mike Porecki was to surprise a kindly community bus driver with a visit from Blakey, who would berate him for bending the timetable by helping old ladies with shopping to their door. We arranged to see Stephen in a tearoom in Shanklin and were a little disconcerted to meet the most gently spoken, grey-haired chap imaginable. Mike and I looked at each other nervously and outlined the plan. 'Ah, I see. I think I understand, chaps,' said the ultra-polite actor, reaching into his bag. Out came wig, moustache and inspector's hat, the demented expression took shape on his face, and the full 'I 'ate you, Butler' voice followed. I quickly developed an admiration I've retained to this day for the skills involved in making what sometimes looks like trashy TV. Sports coverage is a craft, too, but the raw material is there for you – in an entertainment show like *Strictly Come Dancing*, the short film inserts are craft masterpieces and are slaved over every week. That doesn't mean I'm all that likely to watch any of those shows – give me sport or news any day – but I have huge respect for those making mass audience TV[3]. If sport's dull, we can blame the participants, but if an entertainment show's dull, it's a non-starter.

I'm sure some of *Hearts of Gold* was on the soppy side, and we certainly wrung every last drop of sentimentality out of some of the stories. But one in particular was very special to me. Thanks to the wonders of YouTube, I've just watched it again and now appear to have something in my eye … There had been a number of letters from parents and some of their kids in the North East about a pioneering orthopaedic surgeon called Mr Roger Checketts who, along with his team, had devoted his life to improving the lot of countless children whose conditions had previously been deemed inoperable. One of our production meetings watched a rough cut of a quite incredible film about his work. Cynical though TV can be, there are times – as I was later to discover on a *Sport Relief* filming trip to Uganda – when it's impossible not to be overwhelmed by the images in front of you. This was one of those times.

---

3   Though *Strictly*'s wholesome enough, I'm not keen on voting-based shows as a rule. The fun stopped when a reality TV megalomaniac's manufactured contributions were heavily edited to the point where he was seen by millions as a plausible US president.

Our surgeon was going to come on to the show on the pretext of being booked for a medical discussion programme, then be surprised by our film and many of his patients. But what would work as a reward? It seemed as though he'd spent his entire life devoted to his patients. 'He follows a football team, their picture's on his wall,' said one of the producers. 'Well, let's get them on,' said Esther, 'which team is it?' 'Selkirk, I think,' said the producer. I piped up and said it was most likely Celtic if they were wearing green-and-white hoops, and was quickly told that indeed they were. So, as the smart alec who knew their name, I was told to get them to appear on the next show to be recorded on Thursday, 10 November, just under a week away. Hmm, Glasgow to London, a Thursday night, training next day, alarm bells started ringing – 'I'll check the fixture list,' I said.

Now, there was something of (a more liberal) Margaret Thatcher about Esther, and this was clearly one of those situations where she just wanted it to be sorted out, rather than someone bleating about sportspeople and logistics. Instead of simply trying to pull this rabbit out of a hat, for reasons best known to myself I decided instead to make matters worse by pointing out that as a man in his 50s, Roger's real heroes would have been the Lisbon Lions of 1967, the first British winners of the European Cup. 'Well, get them on too,' said Esther airily, as if they all hung out together in Shepherd's Bush every Thursday and just needed to be fetched from a pub around the corner.

My uneasiness at the task I'd set myself turned to blind panic when I looked at the fixture list. Not only did Celtic have an Old Firm match to play two days after the recording, they were going to be in Germany the evening before it for a European Cup tie with Werder Bremen. There was no way they'd ever agree to a studio appearance in London in between. And how on earth was I going to track down the 1967 team in the next few days and talk them into it? Fortunately, a couple of phone calls to BBC Scotland led me to Jim Craig, the Lisbon Lions' right-back, who was by this time both a dentist and BBC radio football contributor. To my enormous relief, he loved the idea, thought it would be a great chance for a get-together, and gave me home phone numbers for the whole team. No one had a mobile back then, and not many had answerphones, so he and I phoned round all the numbers and kept in regular touch with each other. Jim even offered to co-ordinate the logistics of getting all 'the boys' to Glasgow Airport to travel to London together. By the next office day, the Monday, we had eight of the 11 booked. Steve Chalmers was living in Australia, Jimmy Johnstone had a fear of flying, and captain Billy McNeill had proved difficult to track down for the understandable reason that he was now Celtic's manager and had been busy masterminding an 8-0 win at Hamilton Accies at the weekend.

At this point I was grateful for a paternal helping hand from one of the senior producers, Richard Woolf. His desk was near mine in the office – he was an extremely sharp operator who was later to become programme controller at Channel 5 and Sky One – and I was keeping him updated on progress while glibly telling Esther that the crowning moment of a show three days away was all in hand. The truth was that we had a group of genuinely legendary old boys willing to join us but hadn't booked their captain or the current team as promised.

I finally got through to Billy's secretary – they were flying to Germany as we spoke and here was the number of the hotel they were staying in. I left a message, nipped out to the canteen, came back into the office clutching a sandwich and will never forget the sight of Richard on the phone giving me the thumbs-up, before putting me on to Billy himself. He'd called our office back in the middle of his preparations for a European Cup tie, been sold the whole idea by Richard and committed the entire current squad to stopping off in London between their game in Bremen and the Glasgow derby. He said they'd be honoured and humbled to do it, and that they'd fit in with whatever travel plans we needed to sort. This was the second gigantic stroke of luck. What a gentleman, what an ambassador for that 'grand old team'. Even in 1988, that level of co-operation from a man with so much on his plate seemed extraordinary to me but, having never explained how unlikely all this was to happen, I saw no point in telling the rest of the office that Billy McNeill's assent was like a 500/1 winner coming in at the races.

I looked after both sets of players on the programme evening – Roy Aitken, Frank McAvennie and the rest of the modern playing squad were remarkably amenable considering their week's plans had been messed up and rearranged around our show, and that they'd just gone out of Europe 1-0 on aggregate. I can't imagine a modern-day Champions League squad doing anything other than mutinying – possibly through their agents – if asked to emulate them. But the boys of 1967 were something else, ribbing each other, reminiscing and bonding like they'd never been apart. I was particularly thrilled to meet the great Bobby Murdoch, whom I'd watched in awe as he played for Jack Charlton's Boro towards the end of his career – I don't think I ever saw him give the ball away – but they were all humble guys, all from the Glasgow area, who clearly felt blessed to have grown up together and played in Jock Stein's all-conquering team. If you search for 'Hearts of Gold Celtic' on YouTube, you should still be able to see the end result. I'm biased, but it still gives me goose pimples to see Roger Checketts' almost child-like reaction as Esther surprised him with the current squad and then the boys of '67. Billy paid fulsome tribute to Roger's work and invited him to be guest of honour at a game at Celtic Park. The segment went down a storm, and I was flattered to be sought out for a pat on the back after the show by John Morrell, the head of department, and Desmond Wilcox, Esther's husband and a considerable figure in TV production in his own right.

I was learning fast that many of the plaudits and the brickbats you receive in television are for things over which you have no control. An interviewee in the right or wrong mood, a sporting or musical performance which lives up to expectations, or flops, a great or indifferent camera crew or VT editor, can make or break you. In this case, we had the immense good fortune to have dealt with Jim Craig and Billy McNeill, thoroughly decent, unstarry human beings who were prepared to put themselves out considerably to honour a Celtic fan who had excelled in his own field. The next quarter of a century working full time around sport certainly didn't always pan out like that. But once we'd ended that run of *Hearts of Gold* in a blur of wrap parties then Christmas excesses, it was time to move on and try my luck in BBC Sport, the place I'd wanted to work since I was six years old.

I'd been all over the BBC in a 15-month whistle-stop tour, getting all manner of mistakes out of my system, and my timing was fortunate once more. With several producers leaving or about to leave to join the newly formed BSB (which was later subsumed into Sky), the sports department actually needed some extra pairs of hands. I was ridiculously blessed to have served that apprenticeship with Mike Neville, David Coleman and Esther Rantzen and some fantastically talented and dedicated production teams who had been prepared to teach and trust me. I was far from the finished article when I arrived at the *Grandstand* office in Kensington House just off Shepherd's Bush Green that first week of January in 1989, but I was certainly now better equipped to survive than I had been when I first walked into the BBC.

The first BBC Sport studio, as opposed to office, day in which I was involved was Saturday 7 January 1989, a date notable for non-league Sutton United beating top-flight Coventry City in front of the *Match of the Day* cameras in a famous FA Cup third-round giant-killing. Within 100 days, however, the FA Cup was to provide the backdrop to the darkest of all days for BBC Sport, indeed for the whole of British sport.

2.

Hillsborough

15 April 1989. A date which is still painful to type. Nearly 30 years later, that incongruously sunny afternoon in Sheffield regularly comes to mind. And that's despite my never having been in danger, nor knowing anyone who was.

That Saturday in Sheffield also saw the start of the World Snooker Championship at the Crucible Theatre. The first major sports event I'd ever worked on was the 1988 Crucible at the end of my *A Question of Sport* stint. Three months into my attachment to London Sport, I was delighted to be asked to work on the snooker again. I was even more pleased that spring Saturday morning to walk into the snooker production office and be asked if I'd like to help out at the football outside broadcast up the road. It was going live around the world and would be featured at length in that evening's *Match of the Day*. There were more cameras on site than usual and they said they could use some help with the slow-motion replays. 'Count me in,' I thought. 'There's 16 more days of snooker, but this is an FA Cup semi-final.'

I caught a bus from the city centre and joined the expectant throng walking up the Penistone Road, crossing the bridge over the River Don then taking a left turn past the main stand to where the BBC vans were, on the corner by the Leppings Lane end. There was a real chatter in the air – Liverpool were the best team in the country; Brian Clough's Forest were one of the most exciting. They'd played at the same stage of the FA Cup at the same venue the previous year, Liverpool winning an excellent game 2-1. It was all set up to be a cup classic.

I'd been to Hillsborough as a fan and knew how it was configured as a stadium: at Sheffield Wednesday home matches, the Leppings Lane end was divided, with one half reserved for away fans. Control and segregation were paramount in that era. Two central pens (pens three and four, as we now know they were called) were generally kept empty in case the visitors got too near the home fans. However, this went out of the window for a cup semi. Each set of fans was given roughly half the ground so, presumably in order to allow more to get in (and to make more money in the process, of course) the central pens were occupied. The fences running perpendicular to the pitch, which usually kept fans segregated, would, tragically, on this occasion prevent sideward movement for those trapped in these rarely used central pens and the tunnel behind. No one had ever thought to adapt the entry procedures or signage accordingly.

I arrived at the BBC vans at about 1.30pm. The director, John Shrewsbury, was the most experienced football man in the organisation at the time (he was our then FA Cup Final director), my fellow assistant producer in the videotape vans or VT was my contemporary Peter Allden, and John Motson, whom I knew slightly by then, was commentating. We all had a quick cup of tea, found that even the veterans were excited about one of the games of the season, then got into our match positions, with Motty heading up to the gantry while we went into the trucks. I remember Peter and I noticing how relatively empty the corner pens were at the Leppings Lane end, and how packed the two central pens were, but no alarm bells rang. I've subsequently talked to latter-day BBC commentator Steve Wilson, who as a young fan made the trip from Merseyside with a friend. As they made their way beyond the turnstiles well before 3pm, they decided to turn left, rather than go through the tunnel into the central pens ahead. Such decisions were the difference between life and death that day.

The game kicked off, and, as history records, at 3.06pm it was halted. Motty, quite reasonably, asked John Shrewsbury for some tighter shots so he could make sense of what had caused the stoppage. I remember John S, whose judgement was impeccable all afternoon, quietly saying that wouldn't be possible. There was an eerie silence in VT only punctuated by the distant crackle of talkback as the various stunned cameramen and floor managers related what they could see. I don't want to go into the details, but in the videotape area we were fairly certain within a few minutes that people had died.

The cameras were able to capture some of what was happening but were powerless to do anything to help. John Shrewsbury told them to keep recording but never cut any of their closer shots live to air. Many hours later, once our pictures were no longer being transmitted to the world, he made sure everything was sent down the line to Television Centre for posterity. Those pictures, while ingrained in the minds of all of us who were working there that day, have never subsequently been seen other than by the successive official inquiries. The tabloids, of course, had no such compunction, and to their eternal shame (if they had or have any) printed as many graphic images as possible the following day for no reason I've ever discerned, other than to shock and sell papers. The trauma caused to the families and friends of the easily recognised victims was presumably seen as acceptable collateral damage. TV is a far from faultless medium, but it had never crossed the mind of anyone controlling our broadcast to show anything other than wide-angle shots in the television coverage.

At one point in the afternoon, I needed the toilet – the nearest ones were in the main stand, so I left the van briefly. When I returned, I suggested that everyone should avoid going outside if at all possible. Until then, we'd thought that there were a handful of fatalities at most – we feared there were some from the pictures we'd seen – but hoped most of the people we'd seen carried away on stretchers and bits of advertising hoarding would recover. Now I had some inkling of how horrendous this was. There were bodies lined up in a long row – dozens it seemed – right by our vans. There was a makeshift cover for their heads, but the legs and feet in jeans and trainers, some not even adult sized, told of people mostly my age or younger. It's not an image that I will ever be able to dispel, so I can't begin to imagine the effect it had on those who survived, or, as we subsequently learned, the families who found their loved ones lined up in a similar fashion in a gym at the stadium later that evening.

It's still difficult to feel anything other than rage at what unfolded that day. Once *Grandstand* had given way to live news coverage (it had been decided that *Match of the Day* would go ahead with no match action), and to try to make some sense of what had happened, I teamed up with one of our camera crews and reporter Gerald Sinstadt to gather as much material as we could for that evening's programme. Our first dreadful task – by now the ground was empty – was to go on to the Leppings Lane terrace. Again, those images are scorched into my brain: crush barriers twisted and broken into metal spaghetti by the sheer weight of a mass of human beings; all kinds of detritus, and the stench and sight of the involuntary bodily functions which accompany being crushed and suffocated to death.

In the unlikely event that Kelvin MacKenzie or anyone from South Yorkshire Police who fed Kelvin's later 'The Truth' front page to *The Sun* is reading this, that's *involuntary* bodily functions. The teenagers and young people who were amongst the first to enter the ground weren't drunk or ticketless, and didn't urinate on each other or the police, or pick anyone's pockets. Just to be clear, in case the man who, until he likened Everton's mixed-race player Ross Barkley to a gorilla in 2017, was still the star columnist of Rupert Murdoch's *Sun* is interested. Or indeed Rupert himself, for whose corporation football fans have meant decades of vast profits.

We then went to South Yorkshire Police headquarters where the chief constable, Peter Wright, had agreed to be interviewed by Gerald Sinstadt. Gerald was a fine journalist and asked all the right questions, particularly about the set-up at the Leppings Lane end but, as far as I remember, all that came back across the desk was platitudes. The chief constable had been off duty that day and had come into the office once events had started to unfold. It was pretty clear from the interview and from talking briefly to him once we'd stopped recording that he knew next to nothing about the ground, nor what must have been one of the biggest operations on his patch, but it took decades for us all to find out quite how self-serving and incompetent the upper levels of his outfit actually were.

By the time we got back to the ground, the world's media had descended from London and were awaiting the arrival of the sports minister, Colin Moynihan. As someone who'd contemplated a career in news and was still thinking I might end up there, the next couple of hours were instructive. An American network reporter was rubbing his hands together outside the main entrance and congratulating himself within earshot of anyone nearby on his luck at landing a big story on what had started as a quiet news day. When Moynihan's helicopter landed on the pitch, our cameraman (who'd been in the ground, mostly at the Leppings Lane end, all day, and was later treated for post-traumatic stress disorder) was elbowed out of the way by a crew from somewhere or other who seemed to think it was a showbiz press call. An undignified and wholly inappropriate scrum developed. We were in no mood to fight other crews in the circumstances and in the end had to match the sound from our camera with pictures from another camera using a long lens to shoot from the gantry. The minister had only uttered more platitudes, in any case.

As the only permanent TV presence on site, the BBC vans started to receive a string of reporters looking to send their material and find out a few basic facts about an event, and in some cases sport, which was a mystery to many of them. Peter Allden and I tried in vain to explain to journalists and producers that this was nothing whatsoever to do with the 'British disease' of hooliganism. We sketched out the design of the ground and how pressure in the central pens had led to the deaths, but even the distinguished BBC News reporter Jeremy Bowen (who did behave with dignity, unlike some) didn't go down that route. Though he didn't provide much explanation – possibly judiciously that soon after the event – at least he didn't glibly link it all to crowd behaviour as so many others may have chosen to forget they did. All in all, it was a glimpse of the media pack at its callous, sensationalist worst, and I knew there and then that I'd never have what it took to work in news.

For what it was worth, Peter and I, and many others who'd been working for the BBC that day, gave testimony to the first, now discredited, Hillsborough Inquiry. I spoke to two West Midlands detectives for a couple of hours about the live pictures we'd seen, the ground design and how the most dedicated, and mostly young, supporters had died blamelessly in those central pens. I even told them how little the chief constable of South Yorkshire appeared to know about the ground and the operation. It probably all bit the dust along with any other inconvenient testimony.

With the benefit of hindsight, football had been sleepwalking towards something catastrophic for some time. The grounds were in many cases a crumbling disgrace – even the tragedies at Bradford and Heysel in the same month in 1985 seemed not to have made much difference. As a student for much of the 1980s, following Boro around the country, but also attending many big games as a neutral, I took it as read back then that fans were going to be herded like cattle and treated as troublemakers until proven innocent. In return, there was indeed the occasional outbreak of the kind of hooliganism the authorities and government seemed to think was universal. It was something of a vicious circle: if you treat people abysmally, the chances are they'll behave accordingly. The police – notably in South Yorkshire – had effectively become Mrs Thatcher's private army during the miners' strike; there were no camera phones and virtually no CCTV to record egregious acts.

Many football fans had had enough of it all and stopped going to matches. I'd been at Stamford Bridge for the previous year's play-off final where, at best imbecilic and at worst wilfully culpable, stewarding had allowed the Shed End fans on the pitch after Chelsea's relegation to attack 10,000 Boro fans at the other end of the ground. On that occasion, though many of us were shaken up and some hit by stones and other missiles, Ken Bates's militaristic fencing had probably prevented more serious injury. Tragically, the exact opposite happened in Sheffield, where similarly unbreachable fences trapped the injured and dying inside the pens. Hillsborough that day was also noticeably free of any poison in the air – there was no enmity between Liverpool and Forest, and both set of fans had seemingly been in good spirits, looking forward to supporting their teams in a massive game.

I'd experienced dangerous overcrowding at football, too. The Shelf and the terrace below it at White Hart Lane were packed almost beyond belief for Spurs' UEFA Cup Final second leg against Anderlecht in 1984. Incredibly, the game wasn't all-ticket – Mark Turner and I arrived about two hours before kick-off, paid cash on the gate, and only just made it on to the lower terrace. We heard stories afterwards of people who'd been let in through the turnstiles but remained stuck in the concourse. The staircases were packed solid, all supposed gangways had disappeared, submerged under the human tide, and by kick-off it was impossible to move in any direction or even lift our arms. When Graham Roberts equalised to take the game into extra time, we were hurled a long way without our feet touching the ground. I ended up jammed sideways to the pitch for the rest of the evening. At the time, we knew no better so it seemed vaguely exhilarating, but in retrospect it was ludicrously dangerous, and criminally irresponsible of those in charge. The attendance was officially given as a capacity 48,000, but many thousands more had clearly handed over their money in good faith to have their lives endangered. But that's how it was: football fans were basically yobs, and there was no need to provide them with civilised facilities. Standard procedure was to cram them in on the rare occasions there was a big demand, and who cared if they couldn't see the game or were knocked about a bit?

I was vaguely aware of previous Hillsborough stories, too: Spurs' semi with Wolves there in 1981 had apparently been a distinctly uncomfortable experience, and the 1988 semi had led to complaints from Liverpool fans, as much about being given the smaller allocation of tickets as about overcrowding, though the latter had also been mentioned on the football grapevine and is evident in retrospect if you ever see any match footage, especially of John Aldridge scoring at the Leppings Lane end. Not that an inkling of this generally reached the mainstream press, who were all too happy to swallow the government's line on football fans, even to the point of backing their extraordinarily illiberal ID cards scheme, which had been pioneered by voluble Tory MP and Luton Town chairman David Evans. No away fans, and a central registration scheme was proposed, which would mean you could only ever watch one team at one ground. As an exiled Boro fan, and keen watcher of other games, it would effectively have ended my spectating, and was all set to happen at that point under Colin Moynihan. It took the unspeakable events of Hillsborough, and Lord Justice Taylor's subsequent report, for a semblance of respect for fans and concern for their safety to enter the equation. It took an awful lot longer for the families and friends of the dead of Hillsborough to see their names finally cleared.

My admiration for those who fought on behalf of the innocent for so long knows no bounds. I've been in Alan Hansen's company when he's been moved to tears by the coverage over the years, notably when he gave a posthumous award to the tireless campaigner Anne Williams at *SPOTY* in 2013. As programme editor of *MOTD2*, I commissioned producer Dave Purchase's closing sequence to mark the 25th anniversary of Hillsborough in

April 2014. It was a simple scrolling list of all the names, and all the ages, of those who died. In plain black and white, no sound, no frills. As poignant a piece of television as you'll ever see.

I'd been through nothing compared to anyone directly involved, but I still had a moment when I fell apart. On the Wednesday evening following the tragedy, *Sportsnight* showed extended highlights of the European Cup semi-final tie between AC Milan and Real Madrid. I'd finished my snooker shift and was watching BBC One with some of the production team in the Orchard pub in Sheffield. A minute's silence was to be held in the San Siro for the victims of Hillsborough. On a pre-arranged signal, the referee stopped the game a minute after kick-off, the silence became applause, then spontaneously, and very gently, the strains of 'You'll Never Walk Alone' rose on the Italian air in English, right through to the end of that greatest of football anthems. I'm not sure I've ever heard anything more apt, or moving.

3.

Travels with Motty, Cloughie, Stubbsy ... and Godfrey

I have no idea how those affected by Hillsborough found the strength to resume their lives afterwards. I guess many of them never entirely did. Even as one who'd looked on helplessly from the sidelines then covered the aftermath, it altered my mindset.

I was made a permanent employee of BBC Sport in May 1989 once I returned to the office after the Crucible, largely because two or three more of the permanent staff had defected to BSB, and though relieved to finally have some job security I didn't really feel like celebrating.

One thing I had learned was that sport, while it's an escape from the everyday and was, from now on, the permanent source of my employment, was not all that important. Even while still at the snooker, I'd had a quiet word with one of the match directors after a missed red was described by a commentator as 'a disaster for Jimmy White'. No one ever means those phrases literally, but for the rest of my career I tried to nip that kind of hyperbole in the bud.

Fortunately, I'd joined *Grandstand* under the stewardship of a truly great editor, John Philips, who saw sport for what it is, entertainment, drama, joy and disappointment, but, for the most part, nothing more. Together with his presenter Des Lynam, they'd moved *Grandstand* into a modern era of montages and tongue-in-cheek links. Even in the midst of live TV chaos, Des always had a good line up his sleeve. A raised eyebrow to camera, and 'I know you love it when that happens' generally extricated himself and his production team from spooling videotape or an aborted satellite interview. In all the years I watched on admiringly from the videotape (VT) area, then for the short period I spent muttering sweet nothings into his earpiece, the only occasion I can ever remember him looking flustered came at Italia '90. For England's quarter-final tie with Cameroon in Naples, it was decided that Des would present from on site. These days, you can generally book a controlled studio or pitchside position, but back then he was squeezed in at the back of the stand, couldn't hear the production team above the pre-match bedlam and lost his thread during his opening link. Even then, he eventually conjured up a great self-deprecating line: 'See Naples and dry'.

The sport was still centre stage on the Philips–Lynam incarnation of *Grandstand* and was always covered properly, but instead of the straight and starchy packaging of the previous BBC Sport era, you were encouraged to be creative, bring in some music you thought might work and try something different to set up an event. *Saint and Greavsie* had loosened up football preview shows on ITV in the 1980s, and *Football Focus* (still contained within *Grandstand* in those days) had also become a showcase for all manner of creative filming and sequences. Some things worked better than others – the April Fool's *Grandstand* opening in which a deadpan Des intones about the 'highly professional' team on duty as a Laurel and Hardy style ever-building wrestling match breaks out on the studio floor behind him, is amongst the funniest things you'll ever see on YouTube. Even when a good idea didn't entirely pan out, the 'bollockings' – the terrifying hairdryer treatment when things went wrong relayed by the veterans of the 70s and 80s – were replaced with a quiet word of fatherly advice afterwards, having given you full backing to attempt whatever it was you'd dreamt up. Everyone on the production team and technical team loved working for the man we knew as Philippo, and a generation of future editors clocked his methods and tried our best to adopt them when our turn came.

Even the bad cop to John's good, veteran studio director Martin Hopkins was nowhere near the terrifying figure his talkback growl – he made Coleman sound like a castrato – would have had you believe. Like Coleman, though, he liked to test the newcomers. Technology was still in its infancy in many ways and slow-motion replays on site were a rarity. When I joined, on-site replay facilities for cricket matches and even the FA Cup and Rugby League Challenge Cup Finals were either primitive or non-existent. In the latter case, the camera coverage on site was cut temporarily to Television Centre, where an array of assistant producers and videotape operators would play in replays in a sequence often decided by who shouted loudest – 'good on low', 'don't use royal box' and the like would come from young whippersnappers like me. But the replay operation Hoppo (we were almost as imaginative as footballers with our nicknames) would throw you into first was horse racing. I've mentioned the credit you're often given in television when factors beyond your control come into alignment: well, this was the polar opposite. A huge, spooling, ancient recording device in the notorious VT17 channel recorded a race, and the operator (often someone not entirely trusted with proper edits) recorded 'pips' on the producer's say-so at key points in the race. So, pip three might be the water jump on the first circuit, pip 15 might be two furlongs from home and so on. Summariser Julian Wilson would call on site for a particular joining point, usually in the run-in to the finish line, and the machine would fly off to the appropriate pip ready to play in pictures for him to recap.

This was the theory, and once in a while it actually came together. Most of the time it seemed to be disturbingly random, and on one of my first stints Julian wanted us to spin back to the third fence on the second circuit of a two mile and five furlong National Hunt race. I'd clocked the fact that the favourite had fallen there, so had the pip number ready. There was a bit of a rewind involved, and Hoppo was starting to growl, 'Are you on cue, VT?' when the machine shuddered to a halt at what looked like the right point on the circuit. There was no time to double check, so we played it in live on BBC One for Julian to peruse at Chepstow. 'Here they come to the third fence,' he said. 'Phew,' we thought. Over the horses went. All of them, unfortunately, a fact not unnoticed by Julian on the air. VT17, that technological albatross, had taken us back to the third fence on the first circuit and we had no alternative but to play in an entire uneventful lap of the race until we reached the actual incident. This was a far from pretty TV moment and led to a late arrival at whatever sport was next in the running order.

I was summoned in to see Hoppo on our next office day. I'd already decided that if I was prepared to accept plaudits for something like that *Hearts of Gold* Celtic segment which had landed in my lap, I'd better take my bollocking for this, and hope I was still allowed to work on his show. I mumbled about learning curves, 'Sorry, Martin, won't happen again,' and generally threw myself on the mercy of the court. He glowered, said we'd move on, and I left the room like a naughty schoolboy. Within weeks, I'd realised he knew as well as I did that the antiquated VT17 set-up was a form of Russian roulette for any producer, but that he just wanted to know that his new recruits weren't the type who'd try to duck responsibility and blame others. So, again, I'd been lucky to have 'parssed the audition' (sic), as John Lennon once said on a Savile Row rooftop.

We took it for granted in those pre-Sky days, and with ITV having largely abandoned sport outside of football and some boxing, that the BBC had pretty much every sporting contract of note. So much so that the *Grandstand* editor was what we, the viewers, are these days. He didn't wield a remote control as such, but when he said the word, the studio director gave the instruction and the vision mixer wiped from one sport to another. On a Formula One Sunday, Philippo would show the first few laps, leave when the pecking order of the race seemed to be established, go somewhere else, maybe golf or cricket, then come back for the closing stages and chequered flag. Anything in between, say, the race and championship leader spinning off, would be played in from videotape before rejoining live.

Although the mailbag proved you couldn't keep all of the people happy all of the time, it was mostly just accepted that that was how it was. No live stream alternatives on the red button, no updates on the website, nothing. I'd grown up watching coverage of my other favourite sport, cricket, constantly interrupted – Graham Gooch was once left on 299 not out in a Lord's Test against India to go to a scheduled BBC Two afternoon news update and was predictably 300 not out when they came back – and the contractual horse racing commitments played havoc, even with the live coverage of the England v West Indies World Cup Final in 1979. Collis King scored a pivotal whirlwind 86 not out in the first innings, which, as I recall, was almost entirely missed live by *Grandstand*[4], but we knew no better. And Philippo, who wasn't in charge back in 1979, generally had the happy knack – in his case, let's call it a skill – of being in the right place at the right time on more occasions than not.

I loved *Grandstand* and still lament its controversial passing in 2007, killed off by contractual losses and dedicated sports channels having rendered the multi-sport format somewhat redundant. But football was my number one sport and the biggest opportunities

---

4   A marvellous BBC web feature called Genome reveals that *Grandstand* showed highlights of the Scottish Rally, international Rugby League from Brisbane, tennis from Eastbourne and three races from Ascot as well as short bursts of the World Cup Final that afternoon. Meanwhile, BBC Two had Open University programming, an interval (!!) then Bob Hope in *Here Come the Girls* (1953) before the cricket finally went over to Two for the closing stages from 16.10. Even worse scheduling than I remembered ...

were to be found down in the dingy, smoke-filled (most workplaces were back then) basement office of *Sportsnight* and *Match of the Day*. *Match of the Day* only surfaced on FA Cup weekends at that point, but more weeks than not *Sportsnight* had good football content. There were FA Cup replays and internationals, and we were able to show a fair amount of European club football, both recorded and live. Before UEFA started selling collective rights for the Champions League and later the Europa League, you could bid to buy live games from the individual clubs. In my time at BBC Sport, we were largely muscled out of the European Cup, then Champions League – although we did provide host coverage of Barcelona's first-ever European Cup success against Sampdoria at Wembley in 1992, when I was lucky enough to be asked to make the videotape opening sequence – but we often picked up live UEFA Cup games. In my time, I sat in vans in car parks and worked on European ties involving Leeds, Blackburn, Forest, Ipswich, Norwich and Celtic. There were some enjoyable highlights, too – Celtic's run to the 2003 final, Ipswich beating Inter at home, and Norwich winning over two legs v Bayern. But mostly, it was Liverpool.

Admittedly, their armchair following across the country delivered bigger audiences than anyone other than Manchester United, but it also probably helped that two vocal Liverpool fans held key positions in our department (though not at the same time) for most of those years. Dominic Coles, a southern Red with a background in finance, was in charge of the BBC's sports rights in the first decade of the 21st century. We'd lost our Premier League rights with effect from 2001, so he did a deal with Liverpool for live UEFA Cup coverage and we also bought the away games as they progressed. To be fair, it worked out pretty well – we went to Roma and Barcelona for live broadcasts and then brought a quite ridiculous final (a 5-4 win against Alaves in Dortmund) to massive BBC One audiences. Alan Hansen and Mark Lawrenson were enthused, Gary Lineker enjoyed being on site in the big stadiums, and for a fairly new editor, working on Liverpool in Europe and our FA Cup and England deal (5-1 in Munich being our second game of the following season, and something like my eighth-ever live game as an editor) was a phenomenal introduction to staging live match broadcasts.

Then, back in the era when I was an assistant producer, there was Brian Barwick. At least he actually came from Liverpool. These days, you probably know him as the FA blazer who courted Luiz Felipe Scolari, then appointed his 'number-one choice' Steve McClaren and, later, Fabio Capello to the England manager's job. He has acquired a remarkable CV as head of BBC Sport, then ITV Sport and, at the time of writing, chairman of both the Rugby Football League and football's National League, visiting media professor at Liverpool University, *Liverpool Echo* columnist and occasional big event 'Sport on TV' critic for the *Daily Mail*. But when I arrived at BBC Sport, he was the editor of *Match of the Day* whenever it appeared and also of *Sportsnight*.

Brian was a large, moustachioed man (think of the golfer Craig Stadler) and a large presence, with a habit of lying back with his feet on the desk flicking through the TV channels as he spoke to you in his office. His nickname, like Stadler, was the Walrus (but not generally to his face). He had the distinct advantage in our industry of being a big personality – 'once met, never forgotten' – which meant he genuinely knew most people in sport and at the BBC. Brian had the enviable ability to stroll in anywhere and talk to anyone. He was also a good editor, particularly of football, and a shrewd assembler of a team, but excessive modesty wouldn't have been high on many people's lists of his shortcomings.

Brian really knew his football and football history, and although he made no secret of his allegiance to the red half of Merseyside, he didn't take on the *Match of the Day* editorship until the summer of 1988, i.e. after the rather gushing 1987 *Match of the Day Live* I'd critiqued and also after the extraordinary 1987/8 Goal of the Season competition, which had simply featured a shortlist of ten Liverpool goals. In the ensuing years, Alex Ferguson was occasionally heard to mutter darkly about pro-Anfield forces at BBC Sport, a mindset only reinforced when Alan Hansen, with whom he'd had history during his brief tenure as Scotland manager, was recruited by Brian and became the leading pundit in the country. According to Michael Crick's biography, Fergie held Brian responsible for Manchester United never winning Sports Personality's Team of the Year until after he'd left the BBC in 1999, the year United pulled off their unprecedented Treble. That charge almost certainly owes more to Fergie's siege mentality than reality, but some of the seeds of his future feud with the BBC were sown.

To be fair, although Brian could sometimes intimidate some of his team, I rarely had any problems dealing with him. I sought him out when I arrived, confident that he'd quickly realise that I knew my football, too, and, with the departure of several assistant producers to the brand-new BSB, I was given some great opportunities. Sheer persistence – I just kept telling him I'd watched every World Cup game since 1974, and he ought to let me work on it – saw me added as the most junior member of his team for Italia '90. I worked my backside off in our VT area at Television Centre, making highlights edits and preparing analysis for Terry Venables, Kenny Dalglish, Ray Wilkins and co and loved every minute of it.

The most-frequently debated aspect of our coverage of that tournament was how Luciano Pavarotti's recording of Puccini's 'Nessun Dorma' came to be the theme tune. Looking back, it seems an obvious and natural choice, but it really wasn't at the time. Football was, according to a famous *Sunday Times* editorial of the 1980s, 'a slum sport, watched by slum people in slum stadiums', only an elite few in the UK knew any opera arias and nobody in their right mind was going to try to mix the two. Philip Bernie, now head of BBC TV Sport – a cultured enough chap, but no opera buff – was a young assistant producer charged with making a montage ahead of the World Cup draw. He heard someone pick 'Nessun Dorma' on the radio as one of their eight *Desert Island*

Discs and had the inspired thought that the climactic line 'Vincero' ('we shall win') would match arguably the greatest close-up shot in the history of football, Marco Tardelli's manic, wobbly jawed goal celebration after putting Italy 2-0 up in the 1982 World Cup Final. It certainly had the desired 'wow' factor as a combination when it was unveiled for the draw, but after that I'm not sure exactly who was on the committee that eventually opted to make this our World Cup music – Brian Barwick and Des Lynam certainly were, so credit is due to them – but even then, Pavarotti's record company initially refused permission, uneasy about associating themselves with a lowbrow sport. Their eventual volte-face turned out to be a spectacularly good commercial decision for them, as all sorts of unlikely British punters started to snap up opera CDs, as well as an acclaimed creative one for BBC Sport.

As for the football, I made an unusually technical piece (for that era, anyway) with Terry Venables on how England could take advantage of Germany's system of three central defenders in the Turin semi against West Germany, as indeed they did for Gary Lineker's equaliser. Terry recorded a voiceover in his inimitable style – ''ere we see Buchwald and Augenthaler against the Dutch, getting in a right tangle ...' It was all ready to go out after the first semi between Italy and Argentina, but when that game went to extra time and penalties and overran its slot, it was somehow passed on to our colleagues at Wimbledon, who ran it during a rain delay the following afternoon. I was glad it made the air, having worked hard to assemble some relevant examples, but couldn't help wonder what the average daytime Wimbledon viewer made of it: 'I say, Daphne, did you realise that Kohler is an old-fashioned stopper who sometimes finds himself in the sweeper position in this system? One would have thought that Beckenbauer would have preferred a conventional back four ...'

My big break, though, was putting together a Gazza montage (yes, him again) for half-time in the England v Italy third place play-off game, by which time everyone more experienced was out on their feet. I'd made a fairly nifty opening to a game featuring the Italian hosts, spooling through all their matches to find half-decent close-up shots and cutting every last one of them to a sprightly Verdi overture, so I was trusted not to make a complete Horlicks of the task in hand, a celebration of the outstanding young player who had claimed the English public's affection during the team's run to semi-final heartbreak.

The end product was nothing special by modern montage standards, but it was well-researched and caught the national mood. I started it with a quote from the recently deceased Jackie Milburn about the teenage genius, interspersed with Newcastle footage, and cut it to a Geordie tune, Mark Knopfler's *Local Hero* theme. Not the most radical music I ever used, but it worked. I swapped the slow introduction and faster finale around so we could finish with quotes from Chris Waddle, Bobby Robson and Franz Beckenbauer and slow-motion footage of the Germany semi, his second yellow card of the tournament, and tears. I knew it had turned out pretty well, but remarkably it was praised live on the air by Des Lynam and Bob Wilson, and later, to my absolute shock, by the great film producer David Puttnam when he happened to be a guest on the same post-World Cup *Wogan* as Gazza himself. None of which did my standing in BBC Sport any harm as a relative newcomer.

I'd been on a couple of train journeys and had meals around live matches with John Motson in my first couple of years in the department, and he'd discovered that I was pretty much as enthused about the minutiae of football history as he was, so whenever he'd fixed up some filming which lent itself to using the archive, I became his default producer. Back when Allison Pearson was *The Independent*'s witty TV critic, she summed Motty up harshly, if hilariously, in her review of Euro '92. The great sheepskin-coated one had yelped, 'It's delightful, it's delicious, it's Denmark,' as the Danes sealed that most unlikely of tournament triumphs. Allison replied in her column with, 'He's mad, he's mundane, he's Motty.' There was indeed a touch of almost *Rain Man*-like introversion and obsessiveness about John when he was in his preparation zone, especially ahead of a big live game, but he was a sociable and funny bon viveur when amongst friends, which included pretty much everyone in football from any given England manager to receptionists and boardroom stewards at grounds across the country. At the more mundane end of the spectrum, there was a time when he'd allegedly only order tomato soup and steak when on the road, he liked traditional Kit Kats, not chunky ones, at half-time, and he once told some of us that travel was overrated: 'I've been to 57 countries with the BBC, and they're all the same: an airport, a hotel and a stadium.' Then he'd confound his image by disappearing during an international break, to re-emerge having been on a Nile cruise with his wife Annie and full of information on how pharaohs were buried. He also had a recall of music and cinema to rival his command of football trivia. Eccentricities notwithstanding, I was extremely lucky to be paired up with Motty and to benefit from his experience and contacts so early in my BBC Sport career.

Our film-making partnership started in the autumn of 1990 with a behind-the-scenes look at Graham Taylor's early days as England manager. The aforementioned great *Grandstand* editor John Philips had also been a fine director who'd made a classic series of *Sportsnight* films in the 70s about the young Taylor and Alan Durban as they set out on their respective careers in management. Armed with this archive treasure trove, and the access Motty was able to arrange since Graham trusted him implicitly, it was a gift of a film to make. A long-haired Graham pinning up a team sheet at Lincoln intercut with writing out his first England squad; Graham geeing up Ross Jenkins and Luther Blissett at Watford intercut with him chatting as England manager to Gazza at Spurs' training ground and so on. It flowed so well that I'd made something like the first nine minutes without it needing a voiceover or any explanation. Brian Barwick came over and looked at the rough cut – in those days our editing was, impractically, in Television Centre while the offices were some distance away down Wood Lane and across Shepherd's Bush Green – saw it was potentially as good as I'd told him I thought it would be and said he could accommodate a longer duration and lead *Sportsnight* with it.

We later had a bit of a spat when Brian Scovell of the *Daily Mail* was invited in to have a look at some of the interview material, a fairly common practice back then to get a bit of advance publicity for something a programme thought was newsworthy. The *Mail* ran most of the quotes I'd steered them towards, but also included a line from a section which I'd subsequently decided didn't really fit my edit. Brian Barwick and Motty saw it in print, and Brian enquired late in the day whether I should reinstate it. By now I'd given several weeks of my life to the project, staying into the small hours (as *Football Focus* producers do to this day) to make as good a piece as I could. I was knackered and exploded, saying something along the lines of, 'Well, why don't you get Brian Scovell back in here to re-edit the f---ing thing?' Brian Barwick quietly dropped the subject, but I instantly regretted my outburst, thinking my Spielbergesque filming career was over before it had begun. Instead, as Motty told me after transmission, Barwick had been impressed by the way I'd stood up for my piece. And to be fair, when I became an editor in due course myself, I never minded someone having an opinion either, as long as I had the casting vote.

Looking back from well into the generally more enlightened 21st century, BBC Sport was still a bit macho and rough round the edges at that time. The far greater number of women on the presentation and production teams, and greater diversity all round, certainly had a civilising effect in more recent years. That said, it was probably a thousand times worse back in the day if you worked for a tabloid, or during the Keys–Gray era at Sky, and it's always been that way at many football clubs. Peter Schmeichel, a true football great and thoroughly lovely man, but sometimes a bit verbose (in his second language) in highlights punditry, once took me to task. I was pussyfooting around like Sergeant Wilson in *Dad's Army,* saying something to the effect of, 'Would you mind awfully being a tad more concise, old chap?' He laughed and said to just give him a bollocking if I wasn't happy because if he could cope with Roy Keane and Fergie, I wasn't likely to upset him. He had a point. So, while I filed away some of Brian's traits as ones I could never recreate, for better or worse, if I ever became an editor, his assembling of a good team and trust in people with ability was something I did try to emulate over the years.

The last series of *Match of the Day* I edited ended with one of my favourite-ever music items. A couple of months earlier a very talented but undemonstrative producer called Mark Woodward mentioned to me that Jimi Hendrix's back catalogue was now clearable, i.e. it could be used for TV montages, and he quite fancied using 'Bold as Love' to end the season. Completely out of left field – the Premier League football season set to an utterly superb, but slightly unhinged blast of 1960s psychedelia with abstract lyrics about colours. I couldn't really visualise it, but Mark could, so I trusted him, asked him how long the track was so I knew how much space to create in the running order and let him get on with it. I just popped in occasionally to the edit suite (now located more conveniently just across the office in Salford) to enjoy how it was coming together. Mark and his VT editor, Scott Ferry-Collins, were nominated for a Royal Television Society craft award for this masterpiece only to be cruelly denied by a judging panel which included the BBC's golf producer. If only they'd cut it to Bing Crosby's 'Straight Down the Middle'.

Anyway, back to the Graham Taylor film I was allowed to cut for *Sportsnight.* Just as I sometimes wonder if the Gazza Italia '90 montage contributed, in its own tiny way, to the hype and media circus that has enveloped the poor soul ever since, I always feel slightly responsible for Graham Taylor, a true gent, allowing himself to be followed around by a crew as his England tenure unravelled for the *Do I Not Like That* Channel 4 documentary. He came across really well in our piece, for which I was once again given excessive credit within BBC Sport. Motty and I were then let loose on a series of in-depth life and times features on other prominent football figures for the next year or two – Jack Charlton, Jim Smith, Steve Coppell and, most notably of all, the great Brian Clough.

It was the spring of 1991, and Cloughie, who had won everything in the game bar the FA Cup, was closer than he'd ever been to winning it. His Nottingham Forest side were about to play West Ham in a live BBC semi, and Motty was on the prowl. He'd found out that Cloughie was shooting an advert with *The Manageress* actress Cherie Lunghi at Twickenham Studios, got him to agree to an interview via some secret route into the Forest inner circle, and told me to organise it at the end of a morning's filming. Sadly, the drinking which was later to take its toll so badly on the great man's health (Cloughie's, not Motty's) meant that this was advisable. And what a good shout it was: Motty, whom Cloughie clearly loved and immediately started teasing affectionately, cannily introduced me as a fellow Teessider, and after a discussion about the then Boro boss Colin Todd: 'A nice young man, I taught him everything he knows,' and where he bought Barbara's wedding ring (H. Samuel in Stockton High Street, for the record), he asked where we wanted him to sit and off we went.

If the Gazza montage and Graham Taylor were a gift, this was the equivalent of winning the producers' lottery. Our interviewee was absolutely flying: funny and astute right through the lunch break, talking about everything from his playing career to his football philosophy. If you ever see an interview clip, and you still do from time to time, of Cloughie in his trademark green sweater sitting in a brightly lit kitchen set, it's from that lunchtime in Twickenham. I had to stifle several laughs behind the camera as he explained what he and Bill Shankly would have done to modern players' agents: 'I would have held Bill's jacket, and Bill would have hit him.' He then held forth on his preferred style of football: 'If God had meant us to play in the clouds, he'd have put grass up there.' With the advert's crew clearly itching to get on with their infinitely more expensive and elaborate shoot, we cleared off, rubbing our hands together, knowing we had something special in the can. 'How long?' asked Brian Barwick later. 'How long have you got?' I replied. It was so easy to edit – a quick voiceover shot with Cherie Lunghi for Des to explain the location, keep Old Big 'Ead in vision as much as possible, and deploy the odd archive clip to bridge edits or illustrate points. It's not false modesty to say the acclaim we received was entirely undeserved in my case, and even a bit exaggerated in Motty's.

Cloughie was just brilliant – to this day, he's the most charismatic famous person I've ever met. When Martin O'Neill told us years later how motivated he was by the stick he took for being educated and not as skilful a player as John Robertson – 'Oi, clever clogs, your job is to get the ball and give it to Robbo' – you could well believe it. Brian Clough never sat an exam or went on a course in his life, but he was instinctively the most brilliant and unorthodox manager, arguably, of all time. League titles at provincial Derby County and Nottingham Forest, and two European Cups at the latter – it's like a sustained, augmented version of that more recent Leicester City miracle. What is it about the East Midlands, come to think of it?

Anorak that I am, though, what pleased me most about the Clough piece was being the first BBC producer to find a goal from his playing career. To those brought up in an era when even non-league goals are captured for posterity, it may seem incredible that there was no filmed evidence available to us of an extraordinary scoring record of 251 goals in 274 games for Middlesbrough and Sunderland. ITV had a few clips of the tail end of his career at Sunderland from Tyne-Tees regional coverage, but the BBC had nothing other than a couple of Movietone newsreel moments of him playing for England, for whom he had never scored. Brian Barwick, knowing about this hole in the archive and, in retrospect, being quite a crafty motivator himself, set me the task of trying to find something more.

I knew that the newsreel companies tended not to cover league football in the 50s and early 60s but did put together FA Cup highlights. Those were catalogued, and he wasn't in any of them, so I had a look through both clubs' records, made a note of every FA Cup game in which Clough scored and ordered up any rushes – the unedited original match footage – which still existed for any of them. A major problem with those films was that only one camera tended to be present, the reels of film were short, a lengthy change of reel had to take place several times a half, and it was absolute pot luck whether any goals were captured. Undaunted, I booked a viewing room and after several fruitless hours of spooling reached reel six of Stoke 3 Middlesbrough 1 (Clough) from 1958. I would almost certainly have been the first person to open the can and load the film in all that time. A few false starts followed with Boro attacks fizzling out in time-honoured fashion, before eventually a slight figure in a dark kit sprinted out of the Victoria Ground mist towards a camera by the goal, pursued by men in striped shirts. Round the keeper he went – 'Go on Cloughie, put it away, lad,' I found myself thinking as if I'd been transported back to this game from before I was born. Round the keeper, a striker's finish, and away he wheeled, number nine on his back. It was him, it was the goal I'd researched, 'a consolation for the Boro' as the *Evening Gazette* would have described it. It gave me disproportionate pleasure to unearth that goal – it's still the only one by Clough senior in the BBC archive – and Motty and Brian Barwick were also disproportionately and boyishly chuffed. That was working for BBC Sport at its absolute best, being given the time and resources to find something small, but priceless.

The film-making for *Sportsnight* may have been painstaking, but the live Wednesday night show was at times the most frantic, hairy production I've ever experienced. These days, match edits are digital and non-linear, so you can start to transmit something before it's complete and no longer have to physically transfer material from one tape to another. Think of Sky+ or instantly assembling a Spotify playlist, compared to recording programmes on to a VHS or dubbing songs from one cassette tape to another, if you're old enough to remember the latter scenarios. *Sportsnight,* with highlights of England and other home countries' internationals, FA Cup replays and European competitions[5], was the clunking analogue midweek TV sport equivalent of VHS and audio cassettes. In fact, when I first worked on the show in 1989, one-inch tapes were the sole means of recording our material. One inch was a reference to the width of the tape, but the huge metal reel in which it was contained was nearly as large as a car tyre and similarly unwieldy. The technology was as ropey as the rollercoaster theme music was excellent. In 2013 I sat next to Tony Hatch, the man who wrote that very tune, at the wedding of my colleagues Ron Chakraborty and Victoria Goodwin – Tony had been Victoria's ex-neighbour – and told him how his composition, accompanied by studio director Viv Kent's cries of 'Are you on cue, VT?' was still the soundtrack to some of my worst nightmares.

The main BBC One news bulletin was fixed at 9pm back then, with *Sportsnight* in a 10pm slot, half an hour or so earlier than a modern midweek *MOTD.* A few years before I joined, that transmission time had been 9.25pm – I actually don't know how that was achievable on a football night. The edits must have been truly awful and the whole process presumably took years off the lives of all involved. Even with a 10pm start, it was physically impossible to transfer all the action needed for a match edit in time for transmission, so a first-half edit would be prepared while the second half was being played, the second-half edit would be a crude assembly of a few clips (any commentator making an error that needed correcting was an instant public enemy number one to all in VT), extra time would see an even more basic hack, or

---

5   Sadly for the viewers, if less so for the nervous systems of the production team, the great old show bit the dust in 1997 when the FA Cup and England rights were snapped up by ITV.

might be skipped completely if no further goals had been scored, and penalty shoot-outs would be turned round unedited in their entirety.

The VT area was absolute bedlam on an FA Cup night: especially on one particular evening in 1992, when a whole set of fifth-round replays seemed to be heading towards extra time. Genome is sketchy on the details, but Liverpool v Ipswich was definitely one of them. We were in serious danger of running out of both VT machinery and people to log (that is, make notes on each game as it happened) then edit the highlights, but we had a viable lead match which was on the verge of finishing in 90 minutes. Bolton Wanderers of the old Third Division were 2-1 up away to top-flight Southampton deep into injury time – a bona fide giant-killing story seemed imminent. We could transmit the first-half edit at 10pm, cobble together the key moments of the second half and, all being well, that would buy us time to get Liverpool v Ipswich and the other games on the air.

Instead, Barry Horne decided to lash in an equaliser from about 40 yards at The Dell, rude words were exclaimed over talkback and all in VT felt their blood run cold. All, that is, except Paul McNamara, our production team's resident Saints fan who, unaware of what was going on elsewhere, charged out of his edit channel celebrating like Marco Tardelli, took one look at his crestfallen team-mates, turned around and hid himself away again. Brian Barwick in the editorial hot seat was pragmatism personified and said over talkback that he'd lead the show with whatever was ready. I'm not sure I've ever heard an editor say that before or since, but he was absolutely right to do so. I've no idea what impromptu running order we collectively cobbled together, but I do recall Middlesbrough considerately helping VT out in a game never intended to be the main match, by conceding two late goals in normal time to lose to fellow Second Division side Portsmouth at Ayresome Park. Later that season, McNamara again let the side down in VT, this time in a van outside Highbury, by celebrating

Ronnie Whelan's late, late equaliser in our live Liverpool v Pompey semi. That Hampshire connection meant he was very much on his own in wanting the underdogs to be cruelly robbed of a first post-war FA Cup Final appearance.

For that 1991/92 season, Liverpool had been allowed to compete in Europe for the first time in six years. Following the Heysel disaster of 1985 in which 39 people – mostly Juventus fans – had died, English clubs were banned from Europe for five years, with Liverpool serving an extra year for their fans' role in the catastrophe. I wasn't privy to contractual discussions in those days, but with Brian Barwick at the helm, suffice it to say no one was astonished when we landed the live contract with Liverpool for that first season back. They still had box office appeal, even though Kenny Dalglish was no longer in charge and the team was somewhat in decline. They'd won their last league title in 1990 and, inconceivable though this would have been at the time, it's still their last ever, at the time of writing. Having lifted that trophy as captain, Alan Hansen had now retired and has indeed now retired from his second career in television, while in the interim, not only Peter Schmeichel (five times) but his offspring (Leicester City 2015/16) have won the league. Not that the best part of three decades' drought, and Manchester United's subsequent ascendancy, ever worried Alan in the slightest, of course.

Back to 1991, and Liverpool were back in Europe. Not long after I arrived at *Sportsnight*, I was reunited with my old *A Question of Sport* mucker and former BBC Merseyside Liverpool touchline reporter Ray Stubbs. Stubbsy had recently been given a reporter's contract by Brian, and good bloke and good pro though he is, like many reporter/presenters he demands a lot of himself and is prone to occasional bouts of insecurity. Brian reminding him that he'd personally 'taken a punt' on this new reporter role and that 'you're going to be marked on this, Stubbsy' wasn't particularly helpful in that regard. Brian duly announced that *Sportsnight* would run an 'all-singing, all-dancing, Liverpool are back' piece to run the week before the first live game. Stubbsy was the obvious choice of reporter, and I was asked to produce it.

Budgets were a bit more flexible then than they are these days; nowadays, everything you even think of doing is rigorously scrutinised by an accountant and often rejected. Back then, a regal lady called Ella Slack (for years, she sat in for the Queen at BBC dress rehearsals for state occasions) had various mystery pots of money to call upon if a little extra was required on a special occasion. Liverpool's return to Europe was deemed just such a special occasion, so we effectively had a blank canvas. Liverpool had been drawn against relative minnows Kuusysi Lahti of Finland. I phoned them up and within five minutes discovered that the club secretary spoke immaculate English, their centre-forward was a guy called Mike Belfield who'd once played for Wimbledon, and that their ground was regularly used as a landing zone for the World Ski Jumping Championship. 'Stubbsy, terrified, piece to camera at the top,' I thought, little realising how petrified I'd be up there, too, when the time came. And it turned out their only game in the interim was going to be away from home, almost in the Arctic Circle. They were flying and we were welcome to join them. If only every (or indeed almost any) experience of dealing with an English club over the years had been that simple.

So, we had our far-flung opponents segment sorted out, but both Ray – having worked at the Heysel disaster – and I felt we had to visit Juventus as the club had lost so many supporters on that awful Brussels evening six years earlier. We knew that the relationship between the two clubs was now strong and that there was a memorial garden in Turin. Through contacts, Stubbsy managed to set up an interview with Juve's president Giampiero Boniperti, a great ex-player and all-round class act who we were fairly confident would find the right words. Brian, while taking our point, was extremely twitchy about how we'd deal with Heysel, and heaped another layer of pressure on to poor Stubbsy's shoulders. He was now going to be marked for his diplomatic skills as well.

In an attempt to provide the licence fee payer with value for money, I then organised a side trip while we were filming in Turin. Inter were the UEFA Cup holders, and their star striker Jürgen Klinsmann was also shortly to play for the world champions, Germany (they'd just reunited and dropped the 'West'), against Wales in a crucial Euro qualifier. A couple of phone calls, and maybe a fax or two, and it was duly arranged for the day after the Boniperti interview. We could get Jürgen, then as now, a born diplomat with immaculate English, to say the right things about the UEFA Cup and Liverpool, and also give us enough material for a subsequent Germany v Wales preview.

At this point, I should introduce a character I'm going to call Godfrey. A small, rotund, jolly English chap of the old school who wouldn't have been out of place in an Ealing comedy. I was amused, but not entirely astonished, to learn when drinking with him one evening that his early career had included a stint as a circus clown driving a collapsible car. Somehow, he ended up as a BBC cameraman: he'd been on the gantry for the 1966 World Cup Final and had some absolutely fantastic stories to tell. He was our designated cameraman for both the Finland and Italy shoots. He really was good company – we had a lively pre-match Saturday night out in the remote sub-Arctic town of Pietersaari where, for reasons which now escape me (but which were almost certainly related to the contents of a bottle), we took over the door of a nightclub claiming to be English friends of Benny from Abba who were buying the club and wanted to introduce ourselves to the patrons. Stubbsy was particularly convincing in this role, if I remember correctly, and the long Finnish night just flew by.

However, good company though Godfrey was, in common with many men of that generation, he had a rather out-of-date approach to political correctness. When we'd been sent to cover the opening ceremony of the Federation Cup tennis in Nottingham earlier that summer, he seemed to wait for a deathly hush before Princess Diana did the honours, then bellowed out his amused amazement that the current holder of the ceremonial title of Sheriff of Nottingham appeared to be of South Asian ethnicity. Those are not the exact words Godfrey used, and as a member of a generally more aware generation, I tried to pretend not to be with him. He and his sound man later held up an Arantxa Sanchez match on an outside court at the same event when they miscounted the number of games played and tried to dismount the temporary baseline gantry when an even number score was reached, i.e. not at a change of ends. One of them slipped, and since they were connected by leads and headphones which became entangled in the scaffolding, they ended up almost on the court as 'they bounced around like f-ing Zebedee', as one unamused colleague memorably described it.

Anyway, the trip to Finland was a joy, the shoot at the top of the ski jump was spectacular, and off we went to Italy to film at Juve, then interview Jürgen. A tasteful, diplomatic and worthwhile trip to Turin passed without incident, and after an overnight stay we got the map out at breakfast and worked out how to get to Inter's training camp a couple of hours away in the foothills of the Alps. Godfrey and his sound recordist (it was often someone called Mike, to my puerile amusement) said they'd go ahead and get the camera set up. They'd hired their own estate car to carry their equipment, and, like many BBC crew members in those days before widespread speed cameras, routinely drove like the clappers. In Godfrey's case, this may also have been a reaction against the constraints of his collapsible circus past.

So off they went. Stubbsy and I finished our breakfast, set off at our own fairly sedate pace and pulled into the car park of Inter Milan's magnificent Appiano Gentile training complex about half an hour before the scheduled interview. The entire Inter squad was there – Lothar Matthäus, Walter Zenga, Dino Baggio et al – assembled ready to board a luxurious team coach. Just time for Jürgen to give us his interview, then they would be off.

No Godfrey. God knows where he was – he'd probably taken the scenic route via a few laps of Monza. Ray and I stood chatting awkwardly to Jürgen: 'Sorry about this, Jürgen – our crew set off ahead of us, they'll be here any minute.' Just as one of the coaching staff gave the command to give up on the idiot Englishmen and their stupid interview, an estate car careered through the gate and screeched to a halt. A diminutive, rotund and very English figure sprang out of the passenger seat, bounded across to the three of us and bellowed, 'Right, where's the Kraut?'

Such was Jürgen's command of English, we suspected he'd understood, but he gave us a superb interview anyway, shook hands and boarded the coach. What a man! This was confirmed almost 20 years later when he joined the BBC studio team for the first time at the World Cup in Cape Town. I never did get round to asking him whether he remembered that interview and Godfrey's indiscretion.

A quick postscript: Liverpool eventually went out of the competition to another Italian side, Genoa, in the quarter-finals. The Brazilian, Branco, later beating off a competitive field to be the least fit Middlesbrough player I've ever seen (I once sat behind a rather portly Boro fan who was wearing a replica shirt featuring Branco's number 30 and the simple legend 'Lardarse'), scored a belting free kick, as his side cruised through 4-1 on aggregate. Again, Stubbsy and I had been asked by Brian to make the preview piece for the previous week's *Sportsnight*. We had the distinct advantage of being given permission to go with then Liverpool manager Graeme Souness to the city and stadium where he'd starred with Sampdoria, as he ran the rule over Genoa against the reigning Serie A champions, that glorious Milan team, which starred Ruud Gullit and Marco Van Basten. And Alan Hansen, Graeme's team-mate through countless domestic and European triumphs, was coming with us.

Stubbsy and I had the honour of being invited to dinner in Graeme's favourite Portofino restaurant with the two Scots. Along with a late night my fellow editor Andrew Clement and I enjoyed with studio guests Peter Schmeichel and Mark Hughes before a Cardiff FA Cup Final, and a few similar evenings away at tournaments with people like Leonardo and Clarence Seedorf, or the lunch at Marcel Desailly's place I'll describe later, it was the ultimate privilege for a football fan. Largely listening, but occasionally prompting with a gentle question, as two illustrious team-mates opened up, we heard story after story and got a rare glimpse into how truly great teams bond. The fact that Graeme was my boyhood hero and, along with Juninho, the greatest Middlesbrough player of my lifetime, just added to the thrill. We did some filming with the two of them pre- and post-match, I got into the ground early with a cameraman and we got lots of shots of the flag-waving, smoke bombs and singing that helped make Italian football the pre-eminent spectacle it was in the early 90s.

Then the match kicked off. Stalemate isn't the word. Milan were the best team in Europe at that time, but Genoa were a top-five team in Serie A and therefore unlikely to be rolled over easily, particularly in their own stadium. It quickly became clear that both sides would consider a draw a decent, respectable result in the circumstances. Van Basten scarcely touched the ball and there wasn't really a shot in anger in 90 minutes. Graeme told us afterwards that he'd seen countless such nil-nils in Italy over the years – the fans absolutely bought into it, too, and left fully satisfied. Literally honours even.

Sadly, a game like that doesn't make for the greatest preview piece. Channel 4 showed Serie A games live to a sizeable UK audience back then, and though they and the league had given us special dispensation to film at the game that afternoon, we had no other access to match action. So, from the next day, Monday, to *Sportsnight* going out on the Wednesday, I sweated long hours in an edit suite, made as much as I could of the great access we'd had to Messrs Souness and Hansen, the colour material we'd shot and used the match footage mostly as punctuation. Stubbsy worked hard on a script, and though we both felt from what we'd seen that Genoa would beat Liverpool in what might be a less than scintillating tie, we tried to whet the appetite for the BBC live games to come.

After previously enjoying an awful lot of good luck at key moments, I learned the chastening and valuable lesson that you're only ever as good as the material you have at your disposal. As an editor, shows I've been involved with have been feted by the BBC hierarchy or nominated for BAFTAs because they were competent and England won 5-1 in Germany or beat Argentina with millions watching, while excellent FA Cup first-round productions, and accompanying hard work, are ignored, well, because they're Chasetown v Oldham Athletic. So, just as I'd had credit heaped upon me for not making an absolute mess of Gazza's World Cup and a breathtaking Cloughie interview, now Stubbsy and I were arbitrarily 'marked down' for attending a stinker of a football match. 'Making Italian football look dull takes some doing,' spluttered Brian Barwick, 'but you two just f-ing managed it.' 'Cheers, Walrus,' I thought, but didn't say.

4.

A Whole New Ball Game

'The game is over for the BBC as it loses the
key battles for sport on television.'

Headline in *The Independent*, 1998

The Independent was never one of the media operations that had a
vested commercial or cultural interest in running the Corporation
down, so it's probably safe to assume that this was a widespread
perception 20 or so years ago. It certainly was if you were working
at BBC Sport.

'A long slow decline,' *The Indy* said, as it canvassed opinion
within the industry. First up, Brian Barwick, head of sports at ITV:
'It's now about paying the market price for the big sports.' Yep, with
the newly formed Champions League and live FA Cup rights now
at ITV, Brian had left our bridge – he'd become head of BBC Sport
in the mid-90s – and commandeered a lifeboat. A live football-free
1998/99 season later, and having watched his ex-number two Bob
Wilson present the live Champions League and FA Cup Final legs
of Manchester United's unprecedented treble, Des Lynam, then
the BBC equivalent of the ravens at the Tower of London, had
been persuaded by Brian that the commercial water was lovely
and also took the plunge. Formula One had gone to ITV in 1996.

Live Test cricket, a BBC TV staple since the days of WG Grace (or so it seemed) had just gone to Channel 4. Then there was Sky. Rupert Murdoch had openly talked of using sporting contracts as a 'battering ram' to sell the subscription television service he'd launched at the start of the decade. And he was as good as his word. Rugby league, that winter *Grandstand* staple since Eddie Waring's era, moved lock, stock and barrel to the summer, and to Sky, as the revamped Super League. They'd bought swathes of rugby union too and were beginning to move into cricket, paving the way for their later (brilliantly produced) monopoly of the nation's summer sport. And they snapped up the Ryder Cup in the era when serial Great British defeats to the United States had become regular European victories once the continentals had come on board. There's a political metaphor somewhere in there, especially given the Murdoch involvement, but let's move on ...

But far and away the biggest battering ram of all was football. If you were going to ask millions of Brits to subscribe to a satellite television service, you had to give them something they'd never regularly been offered before, and the best bet was large quantities of regular live football. Hillsborough had been the low point of British football in every sense. The Taylor Report had finally insisted that football grounds should adhere to proper safety standards and the national team had caught the imagination at Italia '90 to such an extent that the sport had become something Middle England could openly discuss once again. This was a trend that grew exponentially through the 90s with *Fantasy Football*, hip, latte-supping Serie A coverage on Channel 4, and decent bands like New Order and the Lightning Seeds recording the first-ever musically credible official football anthems.

It was a decade of change for football, but one year in particular marked the pre-eminent tipping point. In 1992 we saw the birth of the Premier League, with more live games than anyone had ever dreamed possible available on Sky, who flogged their subscriptions with the catchy marketing slogan 'It's a whole new ball game'. The subsequent history is often written with an air of inevitability, but it's sometimes forgotten that ITV almost snapped up exclusive live rights. The Spurs chairman at that time, and manufacturer of Sky's Amstrad dishes, Alan, now Lord, Sugar is credited by some with having made sure that Sky upped their offer and saw off ITV. What's even less well remembered is that the BBC enabled Murdoch to clinch the deal by providing a fig leaf of respectability, or a bra for page three, if you like.

The brand new breakaway organisation that was the Premier League was, not unreasonably, rather less sure of itself at its inception than it eventually became. It wasn't going to allow an unproven – and at that time, virtually unwatched – broadcaster to have a complete monopoly of its product (I think rights holders and TV companies were already using that unpleasant expression by then). Yes, Sky could show live games every Sunday teatime and Monday evening in return for their £200m bid, but there had to be top-flight football highlights available to the non-subscription viewer, otherwise the sport could disappear from the wider public's consciousness. The Premier League still believes that to be the case, even in this era of multi-billion-pound contracts, and always sells a free-to-air highlights package in every round of TV deal negotiations. On every occasion but one that package has been bought by the BBC. The next shared TV cricket deal from 2020 suggests that other sporting bodies – yes, even the ECB[6] – may have finally learnt a similar lesson.

Back to the early 90s and enter BBC Sport under its head at that time, Jonathan Martin. As well as talking to Sky, the BBC discussed an arrangement with ITV which would, we were led to believe, have seen *MOTD* return but only as a 1970s-style two-game proposition

---

6   The new cricket TV deal from 2020 sees Test and other England international highlights return to the BBC for the first time this century. Along with ten live games per summer – sadly, unless there's a radical change of plan, that's going to be city franchise-based 100-ball-a-side stuff aimed at viewers who supposedly lack the attention span required to follow the T20 format. Goldfish, presumably.

with all the other action kept back until ITV's Sunday live match offering. Sky would, by contrast, give *MOTD* first dibs at all footage other than their live matches, and, in the end, they and the BBC joined forces with a collective, and ultimately successful, bid for the first set of Premier League rights. For a fraction of the money Sky were paying for the live rights, *Match of the Day*, only able to show the FA Cup at that point, could return to its rightful place in the Saturday evening schedules. It was clearly a fantastic potential coup for BBC Sport, which had lost league football rights a few years earlier, but I remember some of us being distinctly uneasy about the bigger picture. We were all happy career-wise to give up pretty much every Saturday night to work on what promised to be a great show, but we disliked everything Rupert Murdoch represented, not least *The Sun*'s role in Hillsborough and its relentless debasing of the general political and social culture. On a personal level, I was far from keen on the idea of him making inroads into television as well as newspapers and potentially further polluting British life in the process.

Who knows whether that Premier League deal saved the wider Murdoch empire as has sometimes been suggested? On the narrower point of the damage that might be inflicted on broadcasting standards in British TV, I needn't have worried: some Keys/Gray excesses notwithstanding, Sky Sports has always employed excellent journalistic and production values, actually raising the bar for everyone else in coverage terms in many cases. So, too, has Sky News which, unlike newspapers, is governed by TV news impartiality regulations, and is mostly a high-quality journalistic outfit. And it's difficult to say what would have happened to any of us at BBC Sport if the other subsequent live sport losses hadn't been offset by the extra workload created by the Premier League highlights and preview programming.

Despite the worrying rights losses and, at times, hair-raising and anti-social workloads, the 1990s were in many ways a blast for us 20- and 30-somethings at BBC Sport. There were good career opportunities to be had: our deputy head of department,

John Rowlinson, a lovely man and fellow sports nerd, had edited programmes for many years before his promotion and thought I potentially had the ability and judgement to do the same. I was regularly given the Friday afternoon multi-sports programme *Sport on Friday* to edit from the early 90s. The late and much-missed Helen Rollason was the adaptable, low-maintenance presenter of a less-watched, less-high-profile mini-*Grandstand* – part outside broadcasts which were in place for the weekend, part preview show. It was the most fantastic training ground in which to get mistakes out of your system and learn live on the air, and one from which a generation of editors and studio directors ultimately benefitted. In due course, I was allowed to deputise for the regular editors on the occasional, less-high-profile *Grandstand, Sunday Grandstand* or *Football Focus*, and was finally let loose on a *Match of the Day* or two just before being officially designated an assistant editor after the World Cup in 1998.

The one downside, and one which still existed when I was line managing frustrated up-and-coming editors 20 years later, was that these opportunities were seen as a perk and, until you were permanently promoted, you had to juggle them with the day job. So, you'd be in until midnight on a Wednesday working on *Sportsnight,* back in early on Thursday to rustle up a *Sport on Friday* running order then write the script with Helen, take charge of the live show on Friday, be back in for *Match of the Day* until late on Saturday, and maybe go to a live cup game or be in VT to produce a package for *Sunday Grandstand* next day, then be back in the office or out filming for *Sportsnight* again on Tuesday. For years, any shopping, visits to the cinema, or catching up with sleep tended to take place on a Monday. Not that I had any regrets. I'd worked in a normal nine-to-five office in my year off before university and, later in life, saw how worn-out and jaded friends who'd gone into other, often more lucrative, lines of work had become. However anti-social producing TV sport was, it was based on doing something we all loved, so there were no complaints from me. Well, actually, there were lots of complaints, not least from me, and sometimes they were justified but it wasn't the worst way to make a living.

The other big trend in the 90s at BBC Sport was down to the improved technology. Major overseas events had previously seen a small production team go out on the road with the commentators and reporters, while the presentation team – and therefore most of the studio and videotape resources – usually remained back at base. So, I'd been in the videotape area in Television Centre for Italia '90 and the Auckland Commonwealth Games that year but was rewarded with a trip to Split in a rapidly disintegrating Yugoslavia to work in the on-site VT area, adding field events and extra track angles to the main coverage, for the 1990 European Athletics Championships.

I listened in awe one hot Adriatic evening as the great growling presentation director Martin Hopkins and veteran presenter David Coleman fell out on talkback over a missed cue, then bellowed at each other about how useless the other had always been at a volume turned up to 11. The late, great athletics director Martin Webster tried to ignore them as his cameras covered the events, and Paul Dickenson manfully tried to commentate live on the javelin qualifying round while Coleman ranted off-air beside him. By the time we got back to the hotel, our two heavyweight verbal brawlers were in the bar chuckling away at each other. It had been the TV production equivalent of the 'Thrilla in Manila'; the contest was over and the two erstwhile slugging pugilists were now giving each other a metaphorical hug of respect. They were probably the two people I was least likely to confront in my entire BBC Sport career, but to hear 'you couldn't direct f-ing traffic' and 'you've never f-ing listened to anyone, you prat' bandied about was a bit like sneaking into the staff room at school and hearing the headmaster and his deputy head laying into each other. I usually adopted an almost polar opposite approach with presenters and commentators when I was later in charge of broadcasts, but I can't pretend it wasn't entertaining and informative to witness how the old guard did it.

1992, the year of the inception of the Premier League, and in which Sky Sports started in earnest, also saw a sea change in the BBC's big event coverage. The Olympics had been secured by the great city of Barcelona, who'd seen off a challenge from Birmingham (no offence, Brummies, but ...) and the technical team thought it would be feasible to take the entire show on the road. It was a massive success and a thrill to be involved. Martin Hopkins and the production manager, Penny Wood, had taken over two hotels purely for BBC Sport in the nearby seaside resort of Sitges, shuttle buses would take us into the International Broadcast Centre (IBC) in a conference venue directly below Montjuic, an old district on a hill which hosted the athletics stadium and that diving pool whose city backdrop made for some memorable images. Being based in the host city meant that we weren't as reliant as before on multiple satellite feeds going back to the UK, so every sport could be recorded on site and put on the air as needed by editors and studio directors who were able to monitor everything. They could walk a few yards to the VT area to see how packages, or the much-expanded feature-making, were coming along. In short, it was the first time a major international sporting event looked the way a viewer would expect it to look in the 21st century.

With the entire staff of BBC Sport out there, the team spirit was off the scale – previous tensions between 'that lot swanning around out there' and 'those clowns back at base' had duly evaporated, Des and the other presenters loved being in amongst it all, and we could work our backsides off and liaise as well as socialise with each other and the reporters and commentators. There were two shifts – my *MOTD* and *Sportsnight* team were on duty early, with the *Grandstand* team working late. I've never been an early morning person, so the daily 6am shuttle from Sitges and 6pm finish sounded like a bum draw until we thought about it more carefully. Back then, the sporting authorities weren't used to a whole team descending from a foreign media outlet, so the same accreditation that got you into the IBC also usually gained you entry into the events. By the time the athletics started in its traditional second-week slot, those of us who fancied it dashed up the hill after our shift, found some observer seats – that is, not for public sale – sat on each other's laps or sneaked in next to the BBC commentary box if necessary, and drank it all in. There were even free sponsors' alcoholic and non-alcoholic beverages available in the media room. I was two seats from Coleman when he called Sally Gunnell home in the 400m hurdles, and as Carl Lewis won his third long-jump gold and his US relay team smashed the world record. Athletics was always up there with football and cricket for me when I was a kid – it still is, despite some of the clouds hanging over the sport – so this was 'pinch yourself' time.

The other joy of the early shift, especially as a 27-year-old, was being free to socialise. The late shift could spend their mornings by the hotel pool, but I wasn't too bothered about missing that. As anyone who's been there knows, the whole of Spain eats late, especially in summer, so you could watch the athletics, catch a bus back to Sitges, get something to eat, then stay up into the small hours with a cold beer or two. OK, you had to be on a bus again at 6am, but we were young and stupid, and there was plenty of coffee available. On the night of my colleague Andrew Clement's birthday, a gang of us, including rookie reporter and Barcelona deity Gary Lineker, went for an excellent meal just off Las Ramblas, played pool into the small hours (Lineker, a snooker century-break man, nonchalantly thrashed all-comers, naturally) then went on with some of our team of local translators to a succession of more and more exotic clubs, one of which opened at 4am and served hot chocolate and churros doughnuts. All hopes of getting back to Sitges long since abandoned, those left (more or less) standing went straight back into the broadcast centre for the morning shift. Our valiant, marginally more mature, team leader Graham Wellham took one look at us – and maybe had a sniff of the fumes wafting off us – and hid us on the sports least likely to make the air.

As at all major events we covered in those times, there was a quotes board up and running. Commentator Colemanballs, production team double entendres or witty put-downs, they had to be good to make the cut. One I seem to remember from that morning was 'I dreamt that I was logging the sailing. Then I woke up and found I was.' Only rivalled in terms of sailing quotations by the quietly sardonic producer Gerry Morrison. He'd been logging away for hours one slow afternoon when a surprise announcement came from the gallery that we were going across live to the closing stages. 'That's a shame,' muttered Gerry, 'they've just missed the leader being dragged down by an octopus.'

The USA World Cup of 1994, spread across that vast country, and with no UK team present, was deemed too complicated and expensive for a similar on-site operation, so again, as one of the main match highlights cutters and montage makers, I was in London. My main memory of that tournament was being asked by Brian Barwick to make a montage to 'Nessun Dorma' as a Roberto Baggio-inspired Italy marched to a final they would eventually lose to Brazil on penalties. I was a bit nonplussed by this, thinking there wasn't much more we could do with this wonderful, but, by now, slightly hackneyed piece of music. Again, just one simple idea made the breakthrough. And it wasn't even a new one. There were far fewer close-ups and isolated angles available in football match coverage then than there are now, so we used to spend a few hours searching through match footage and compiling anything that might be useful before going into any edit. I couldn't help but notice as I spooled that the Italian close-ups often involved mouthing words aloud, combined with expressive gestures and facial contortions. I hope that doesn't sound like a cliché, it just happened to be true. In particular, there was one long sequence of coach Arrigo Sacchi hollering from the touchline, which I could see would work instead of the great Tardelli shot for the final 'Vincero', and an excellent cutaway of an Italian fan in full regalia bashing two cymbals together, which could accompany the short orchestral blast that ends the piece. It was then just a case of lip-syncing and slowing down some of the other close-ups so that the vowels matched open mouths, which then closed on the consonant sounds. There were more than enough of these shots to cover Pavarotti's entire vocal.

From memory, it took the best part of a couple of days to put it together, which is a long time for a minute or so's sports sequence, so thanks to the rest of the team for indulging me, but the end product still looks better than most laughably dated montages of that era, including plenty of mine. At the time of writing, it's on YouTube. I'm not sure whether or not the poster should have put it there, copyright-wise, but we've all paid our licence fees, haven't we?

Having worked on programmes which were nominated for BAFTAs – and having sat on a few sports awards juries myself – I've learnt to take industry gongs with a huge pinch of salt. That is, with the notable exception of the unimpeachable international jury of the 1994 Sportel Awards, which gave that Italian montage a richly deserved Golden Podium for 'absolute genius in the creative arts'. I've lost the citation somewhere over the years, so am paraphrasing somewhat, but that was the gist of it, I believe. I wasn't allowed to go to Monaco to pick it up, though. In fact, I didn't even know it had won until someone from BBC Worldwide plonked a statuette on my desk with a handwritten note thanking me for giving him the chance to meet the glamorous French tennis player Mary Pierce, who'd handed it over to him at a star-studded gala on the Riviera. Then again, Marlon Brando didn't pick up his best actor Academy Award for *The Godfather* in person, nor did Bob Dylan turn up to collect his Nobel Prize for Literature. And those are proper awards. No grown-up should take any of it entirely seriously.

Euro '96 came next – a home tournament in which England suffered more semi-final shoot-out heartbreak. The 4-1 win over the Netherlands, with Shearer, Sheringham and Gascoigne displaying peak Dutch levels of technique and swagger, was probably the best competitive England display of my lifetime. Sadly for us, ITV showed that one live. Many other games around the country were surprisingly poorly attended, though. I have stronger memories, strangely enough, of the 1995 warm-up tournament, the Umbro Cup, featuring a glorious young Brazilian team. Two new players in particular caught the eye alongside the original gap-toothed Ronaldo as they effortlessly dismantled Sweden, Japan and England to lift the trophy. Almost unbelievably, one of them, the diminutive gazelle-like dribbler Juninho, was playing for Bryan Robson's newly promoted Middlesbrough by the end of the year. And the other, the great attacking left-back Roberto Carlos, was all set to come to Boro in 1997 until a points deduction fiasco saw us relegated and also lost us Juninho's services temporarily to Atlético Madrid.

Brazil being in town also led to our acquisition of Pele as a studio guest for the England v Brazil highlights show. I'd got the nod to meet the great man at the stage door at Television Centre and tried not to gibber too much as I looked after him pre-show. I was known to get sniffy in later years if anyone on our team ever took selfies with illustrious guests, say, at *Sports Personality of the Year*, as I always felt our studios should be a hassle-free sanctuary for visitors, but on this occasion professional discipline rather broke down. Someone had brought a camera with them, and at the end of the show pretty much everyone from the VT area descended on the studio floor in the manner of a good-natured version of a *Simpsons* pitchfork-wielding mob. Pele had seen it all before and was a model of grace, good cheer and patience.

For the BBC, Euro '96 was another case of a presentation team on the road, going from game to game, and another – the one of which I was a member – making all the match edits and montages in Television Centre. I do recall that our guest pundit Ruud Gullit, booked by our new editor Niall Sloane, was a roaring success – his memorable line after the great Peter Schmeichel was caught out trying to be an outfield player against Croatia was 'the goalkeeper is only the goalkeeper because he can't play football' – and that 'Walk Away' by Cast worked rather well as Stuart Cabb's closing montage music when England reprised their 1990 semi-final penalties heartbreak against Germany. I am someone for whom annoying behaviour can spawn a decades-long grudge and I distinctly remember Chris Evans, who at the time had positioned himself as Gazza's best friend, tearing up his tickets for the Wembley final live on *TGI Friday* after England's exit. It was an outrageously selfish and arrogant act. He could have given them to any of the ticketless German and Czech fans who came to London on spec that weekend, but no. That, along with certain politicians and others who felt they ought to pretend to like football, as so brilliantly parodied by John 'Soccer!' Thomson in the *Fast Show,* was something of a counterpoint to the 90s football boom.

The next major overseas event after the 1994 World Cup also took place in the United States: the Atlanta Olympics of 1996. Because it all took place in one city, the whole show went on the road again, Barcelona-style. Barcelona it wasn't, though. As is now well documented, not least in its election results, the United States is effectively two countries. Broadly speaking, people living on the two coasts (and, having been there, I'd also include Chicago) tend to be more worldly, widely travelled and liberal than those living in the so-called 'fly over' states in between. Atlanta, while it was a large city, home to CNN and Coca-Cola, and relatively diverse and modern compared to much of the rest of the south, struggled as it hosted the world's athletes and media.

A few examples: a group of us were greeted with astonishment, and a lengthy attempt to dissuade us, by a white taxi driver when we wanted him to take us to Martin Luther King's boyhood home, by then a national memorial. A waiter, on learning we were from Britain, announced he wanted to come and see our Eiffel Tower. The GB rowing team's official transport bus spent two hours looking for the Lake Lanier venue one morning, a US v Argentina basketball match was held up for ten minutes because someone switched the lights off, and I watched the great Frankie Fredericks explain patiently and at length to local reporters that Namibia was a country not a city, and that, no, Africa was a continent, not a country. That's why he was wearing a Namibia, not Africa, tracksuit. The wider media dubbed Atlanta the 'Glitch Games'. I saw it more as the Deputy Dawg Olympics and was just waiting for a security guard to exclaim 'sooey, Muskrat' and call us 'varmints'.

Officialdom, especially the security personnel on duty, displayed superficial good manners while saying 'no' to pretty much anything and everything to such an extent that the UK media dubbed them the 'Nice Day Nazis'. I put my bag down at my feet in one press room, but because it was just on the other side of some arbitrary line painted on the ground, I was sent out of the room, down the corridor and through a door at the other end, and an accreditation check, to retrieve it. It was a good job my accreditation wasn't in my bag, or I might well have been deported. There was a horribly garish, and nakedly commercial Fan Zone we were obliged to walk through between the media hotels and the International Broadcast Centre, presumably in the hope that we'd want to buy some tat before or after a day's work. Tragically, a pipe bomb went off there and killed someone one evening, so the next day massive detours and delays were in place. As we were all making our way slowly towards the IBC, a further detour was announced because another suspicious package had reportedly been found. This rerouting now took us back down the outside of the Fan Zone's perimeter fence, approximately six feet away from where a bomb disposal squad was working on the self-same suspect package, which had been discovered resting against the inside of the very same temporary wire-mesh fence we were now walking alongside. As Mark Lawrenson might have said, 'Reassuring. Not.'

It wasn't a particularly auspicious sporting event, either. Great Britain – I'm old-school, so I try to avoid the ghastly expression 'Team GB' – only won one gold medal, which went to the rowers Steve Redgrave and Matthew Pinsent. My contribution to the end-of-Games review was a music item of British misfortune cut to 'Don't Look Back in Anger' by Oasis. Amongst dropped batons and other mishaps was a memorable shot of defending champion Sally Gunnell pulling up injured while her rivals sped past – 'So Sally can wait, she's knows it's too late' indeed. Britain's paltry medal haul led directly to the introduction of National Lottery funding for elite sport the following year, and we've never looked back as an Olympic nation. Elsewhere, the highlight for me of the Atlanta Games was getting into the Olympic Stadium to watch Michael Johnson's extraordinary dismantling of the 200m world record. His time of 19.32 was widely seen as a mark that might never be bettered. Then again, we didn't know about Usain Bolt. He'd only just turned ten in 1996.

My other memories of Atlanta largely centre around a chap called Carl Hicks. Carl comes from Widnes, is fiercely intelligent and had been a proper newspaper journalist, responsible for a celebrated headline about a spectacularly unsuccessful local rugby league team, which parodied a car advert of the time, 'If only everything in life was as reliable as Runcorn Highfield'. He knows more about more sports than anyone I've ever met and was soon to be the editor of *Grandstand*, but at this point he was a sports assistant, effectively chief stats man to Des Lynam. Carl did have a bit of a temper when pushed – he'd chucked a pen at Brian Barwick and called him various names in a spat early in the Games, which was brave, possibly foolhardy, but quite funny – and, like me, he was struggling with the 'Nice Day Nazis' and all the patriotic jingoism we were witnessing, not least from the domestic Olympic broadcaster NBC. Their coverage would simply abandon any event the American competitor wasn't winning, and colleagues who watched the men's 400m final in a bar were unaware that Britain's Roger Black had won silver because the coverage only showed and mentioned (the admittedly peerless) Michael Johnson winning the race. In the end we channelled our feelings into supporting anyone but the Americans in pretty much any event, although Johnson was generously given special dispensation. Even before he became as great a pundit as the BBC has ever employed, we knew he was a class act.

We were working on the early shift again, so one evening Carl and I went to the USA v Cuba volleyball game, held in an arena right by the IBC. This was an absolute bearpit – God's Own Country v the Commies – and in distinctly un-Olympic fashion, the announcer was soon whipping up the home crowd. Even the scoreboard produced mock firework displays and the legend 'GO USA!' after every home point, but only a simple 'USA 1, Cuba 1' if Fidel's Fiends dared to respond. Cuba won anyway, much to our amusement. We then decided to try to entertain our VT team on the late shift by going into the unused BBC commentary booth at a Brazil v Poland game and providing a not-for-broadcast commentary in the style of Alan Partridge, who at this point was still the sports reporter on *The Day Today*. Some of this nonsense was captured for posterity in the end-of-Games in-house montage, but we got our richly deserved comeuppance when, hollering along and bouncing around between points to the PA's blast of 'Twist and Shout', we were cut up on the world feed. Our ridiculous, uncommentator-like antics were broadcast live to Brazil, Poland and anyone else who was taking the live pictures. I half-expected to be stopped in the street in Warsaw at Euro 2012 or Rio in 2014 and asked about it, but I've lost most of my hair since then so no one pieced it together.

Two final fonder memories of Atlanta – our producer colleague and veteran musician (we knew him as the sixth Stone because he'd once been in a band with Bill Wyman) John Graham had a contact at the House of Blues, a converted church which was now a music venue, and we went to see Bob Dylan[7] play two nights running and a cracking incarnation of the Blues Brothers Band with

7 Atlanta saw possibly the only use in history of a Bob Dylan track on a sports music item. My colleague Asmi Ahmad made a white-water canoeing montage and took up my suggestion of cutting it to the great man's 'Watching the River Flow'.

James – standing in for his brother, the late John – Belushi, Steve Cropper and Donald Dunn from Booker T's band the MG's, and Eddie 'Knock on Wood' Floyd. Whatever else the Americans do or don't do well, music of that ilk is generally phenomenal, especially live. And on the last night of the athletics, Carl and I went to the stadium, where he had a final monumental row with a ludicrously officious and pompous 'Nice Day Nazi' who threatened to have him arrested for standing on the wrong paving slab, before we saw Donovan Bailey, the individual 100m winner, run an anchor leg as if he were on a Harley-Davidson to overhaul the US, silence the baying home crowd, and snatch the 4x100m relay gold for Canada. Marvellous scenes.

The last major sporting event of the 1990s saw a football tournament finally covered in the way the two Summer Olympics of that decade had been. Niall Sloane, previously assistant editor to Brian Barwick, had been promoted to editor when Brian became head of sport. By the time the 1998 World Cup came around, Brian had moved to ITV as their head of sport. In the resultant reshuffle, I'd been appointed assistant editor to Niall, with the move delayed until after the World Cup. This was to be my final stint in VT, and a last hurrah with no overall responsibility beyond my own segments of the output. Honour though this impending promotion was, it really felt like we were nearing the end of an era. Sports rights were haemorrhaging to Sky and ITV, including those to the Champions League, FA Cup and England games and, though we didn't know it at the time, we were shortly to lose Des, the Premier League highlights and some of our best producers to Mr Barwick and ITV. I don't think any of us would have believed BBC Sport would still be covering so many big events two decades later as we approach the 2020s, so both the calendar and the mood strongly suggested 'fin de siècle'. And where better to stage it than Paris?

Niall was determined to find a studio setting in Paris, and eventually secured the top floor of the prestigious Automobile Club de France on the Place de la Concorde with a roof terrace overlooking various Parisian landmarks, and with the Eiffel Tower in the distance. With Brian now in charge of our rival's output, the competitive edge which always existed with ITV had ratcheted up. Having Des and pundits based in a hotel five minutes' walk from the studio gave our coverage a distinct advantage over ITV, who were presenting on the road from a succession of noisy, sweaty stadiums. One of our regular *MOTD* production team, Asmi Ahmad, oversaw some glorious opening titles shot in the beautiful Art Nouveau Brasserie Julien on Rue de Faubourg – some of us have been back several times since – so between those and the opening studio shot, the viewer was left in no doubt where we were based. Paris ran through the shows like the lettering on a stick of rock.

Niall had also worked hard at assembling a studio team with familiar *MOTD* faces in Alan Hansen, Mark Lawrenson and the soon-to-retire Jimmy Hill, alongside Ally McCoist and an inspired signing, Niall's fellow-Ulsterman Martin O'Neill. Martin had played in the 1982 World Cup (as had Alan Hansen) and was by now one of the hottest young managerial properties in the game at Leicester City. He'd even won a League Cup Final with them. Against Middlesbrough, naturally. The sprinkling of exotic stardust and a real coup at the time was the signing of David Ginola. He was French, good-looking and a key figure in the snowballing glamour of the Premier League. He'd lit up Kevin Keegan's exciting Newcastle team and would be voted PFA Footballer of the Year during the following 1998/99 season at Spurs but wasn't involved in the tournament as a player. He'd been controversially omitted from the French squad ever since national coach Gerard Houllier blamed him for the concession of a Bulgarian goal which led them to fail to qualify for USA '94.

My first encounter with Ginola was a memorable one. He arrived at the studio a couple of hours before the Brazil v Scotland opening game, and as Niall showed him around he suggested that David might like to watch the Brazil montage I'd been making for transmission pre-match. I'd had an idea in my head for years, based on one of the greatest singles of the punk/new wave era, 'Another Girl, Another Planet' by The Only Ones, and since this was going to be my swansong in VT I'd finally been given the chance to put it together. It had occurred to me that pretty much every lyric in a slightly spaced-out song of love and awe could apply equally to our extensive archive of Brazilian World Cup moments. The most problematic line – 'I won't need rehabilitating' – had been solved when I stumbled across a shot of Diego Maradona in a Brazil shirt he'd swapped after Argentina eliminated them at Italia '90. Substituting one of those excitable Brazilian commentators screaming 'Gooooaaalll' for 'girl' when the title line was sung, it became 'another goal, another planet' and since this was immediately followed by one of the greatest extended, soaring guitar solos in rock history it provided an irresistible excuse just to cut together every great Brazilian World Cup goal we had in the archive. It was difficult to go wrong, and since I can't track that one down on YouTube, it's even easier to say glibly that we didn't. David watched this orgy of glorious football nostalgia in silence, smiled broadly, then hugged me. Which was nice, as they also used to say on the *Fast Show*.

We did have a few slightly starry moments with Ginola. It transpired once we'd crossed to the first half of that opening match that his agent, possibly not understanding our concept of punditry, had booked him to appear live on French television across Paris at the end of the game. Niall's generally affable tone degenerated somewhat as he explained firmly that David was going nowhere. We half-expected our burly floor manager Chris White to have to rugby-tackle him to prevent him from leaving, but fortunately it didn't come to that. Thereafter, juggling various media and sponsor commitments, he tended to arrive rather later and somewhat less prepared for the broadcasts than his fellow pundits, even falling asleep during one game, and he was duly dubbed 'Diva Dave' by Hansen and Lawrenson, whose Anfield boot room ethos disapproved of any hint of superstar behaviour. Ultimately, though,

he was charm personified on the air and a huge asset who, as Gullit
had in 1996 and as Leonardo, Klinsmann and Seedorf and others
would at later tournaments, helped to make our coverage look
considerably less parochial than might otherwise have been the
case.

In the aftermath of France's memorable tournament victory and
with a multi-racial French nation pouring on to the streets in their
hundreds of thousands to celebrate their rainbow team on the Place
de la Concorde outside our studio, I did spare a thought for David
Ginola. He'd been gracious on the air that evening, but in some
ways, albeit for different reasons, he was now his nation's Jimmy
Greaves, watching their historic triumph from the sidelines, while
presumably feeling somewhere deep down that he should have
been out there playing. He's actually followed a similar subsequent
career path to Greavsie. During Euro 2016, having landed a ticket
in the UEFA ballot to the Spain v Italy game, I was in Paris the night
England were knocked out of the tournament by Iceland, only days
after our EU referendum vote. I sat in a bar watching David host
the French TV coverage with a panel of French ex-Premier League
players trying to make sense of it all. Unlike the Italians, Spaniards
and French in the bar, he manfully refrained from dissolving into
laughter, pointing at the screen and chanting 'Brexit, Brexit'.

Six weeks in Paris – slightly longer in my case, because I'd
arrived early to produce our tennis commentators at the French
Open – gave us the chance to get to know the other pundits better.
We saw quite a lot of Alan Hansen and Mark Lawrenson in the
videotape area back at base around *Match of the Day*, and Gary
Lineker was by now our number two, soon to be number one,
presenter, but Jimmy Hill was being used less and less often by
then, so the impromptu team meals we had in a succession of Paris
brasseries was the first chance I'd had to spend much time with him.
My previous limited contact with him had mostly come when we'd
travelled en masse to live FA Cup games. In particular, I remember
stepping off our coach just behind him at Maine Road for a Man

City v Spurs tie in the early 90s. Jimmy was a bit of a pantomime villain to supporters of certain clubs, his fearless style and strong opinions having occasioned a perceived slight or two, and there was a torrent of abuse – some good-natured, some less so – as he emerged into the light. He paused, smiled and waved as if it was a royal visit, and said, 'That's fame for you.' It turned out this wasn't the first time he'd used that line – Des tells of a similar moment walking round the pitch with Jimmy pre-match at Goodison Park – but as a way of dealing with vitriol, it takes some beating. Jimmy would have coped just fine in the social media era.

Like Motty in later years, Jimmy embraced the fact that his public persona was a somewhat eccentric and easily caricatured one and had cheerfully involved himself in stunts like Des and Alan Hansen blowing him up on the *MOTD* set for a classic *Comic Relief* sketch. But there was so much more to him than that – as a Fulham player and PFA chairman, he'd helped abolish the outrageous maximum wage rule which had prevented star footballers from sharing in any of the bountiful gate receipts they'd generated prior to 1961. He later managed, then became chairman, at Coventry City, dragging them from the old Third Division to three decades in the top flight. In the process he'd instigated all-seater stadiums, electronic scoreboards and the transformative three points for a win which achieved his objective of making chasing victory more appetising than settling for a draw. As a broadcasting executive, he'd overseen ITV's innovative and ratings-boosting World Cup panel format in 1970, then joined the BBC for more than a quarter of a century. An extraordinary legacy. He may have seemed a bit old school by 1998, and occasionally expressed one or two old-school opinions typical of his generation, but he really had lived a life and was an avuncular and fascinating dinner companion.

At the other end of the longevity scale, there was Martin O'Neill. He was to work regularly with us over the coming seasons – and developed a close friendship with Niall Sloane. Even so, he had a thing about unsuccessful managers working as pundits, and never signed up for tournaments until the last minute. That is, until he was sure that his recent track record still made him credible. He was brilliant company – his Clough anecdotes alone held us spellbound – but had a wide-ranging hinterland of books, films, and as a former university law student, famous criminal law cases. His wife and two daughters joined us at tournaments and became a regular fixture on our social scene. I have fond memories of Andrew Clement, armed with a guidebook, trying and failing to find an obscure recommended restaurant in a far-flung corner of Paris, as we walked for miles in the rain with the whole O'Neill clan cheerfully in tow, showing no signs whatsoever of starry disgruntlement. One of the first things Martin did when he joined us in Paris was to tour the studio and VT finding out what everyone's role was. He learnt most of their names, asked smart and sympathetic questions, and had everyone on his side within hours. You could see why he was succeeding in management – we'd all have run through a brick wall for him by the end of that tournament.

As a current coach, Martin was a fine on-air dissector of football, but his never-to-be-forgotten moment in Paris had nothing to do with the game itself. One Saturday lunchtime live game was already in progress, with Niall in the gallery and the team on the set, when our production manager Patricia Gregory popped into VT and said, 'we have a visitor'. As the only vaguely editorial figure present, I was summoned to the door where just about the most famous man in Britain at that time was standing. Robbie Williams, a genuine football fan who'd put in the hard yards following Port Vale, was on a visit to Paris, and had rocked up in a 'Des is God' t-shirt. Unlike the young Gazza back at BBC Newcastle, he was expecting to come on the show, so at half-time Des introduced him and a jolly chat about how he was enjoying the tournament ensued. Now, among his many other non-sporting passions, Martin O'Neill knew a lot about music – we'd already discussed favourite Small Faces and Led Zeppelin tracks long into the Parisian night as he light-heartedly took issue with Hansen's Billy Joel and 70s soul obsessions. It was in a similar mickey-taking vein that he started out of nowhere on Robbie. A couple of minutes later and the boy Williams was on the ropes as Martin enthusiastically informed him that he'd got lucky and that Gary Barlow was the real talent in Take That because he wrote the songs. It was brilliant, unscripted and slightly unhinged television.

The 1998 World Cup was a triumph for the BBC, and for Niall, in charge for the first time, in particular. Even those who normally sharpened their pens to accuse the BBC of being complacent, stale or worse had to admit that this one had gone pretty well. And yet, in the upper echelons of the BBC, in places I was yet to encounter at close quarters, there was a gnawing sense of disappointment, related to something I quietly found even more inexplicable than the collective anxiety about awards. I've already alluded to it in my reference to Jimmy Hill and the 1970 ITV panel: audience figures.

One of the great joys of working at the BBC, rather than, say, ITV, is the absence of adverts – just ask Bob Wilson, Des Lynam or Adrian Chiles. I was always grateful, especially as an editor, that 'the unique way the BBC is funded' meant no interruption between the teams coming out and the game kicking off and gave us the chance to fill half-time and full time with extended analysis, features and recaps. Even as a fairly aware viewer, though, I'd struggle to tell you which England and other games I'd watched live on the BBC and which on ITV during the 1982 and 1986 World Cups. Clearly, you'd watch a big game wherever it was being shown. The only time you'd be forced to choose was on the rare occasions when the two channels went head-to-head, usually for cup finals. We'd tended to be more of a BBC household when I was growing up, but if we happened to be watching on ITV, we'd switch to the BBC whenever adverts appeared, and more likely than not stay there. Hence, for the most part, the natural ratings advantage for the BBC.

Yet, somehow in the willy-waving world of television scheduling, these figures meant everything to our bosses. This made some sense at ITV, whose advertisers needed to know how many viewers they were reaching, but rather less so, I always thought on the quiet, at the BBC. Clearly, it's difficult to justify the licence fee spend on sporting events without the healthy audience figures they generate, but since the rights fee for, say, a World Cup was divided between the BBC and ITV, it ultimately made sense for both channels to do reasonably well out of the deal. In theory, either channel had the right to show whatever live games it wanted, but a sensible compromise involving alternate picks (rather like selecting teams in the school playground) provided balance and avoided alienating the non-sports general audience entirely. It was always accepted that both channels would show a final, and that the lack of adverts (or, if you were a blinkered chauvinist, the innate superiority of the BBC) tended to make that a one-sided ratings contest. At the home nation-free Euro 2008, ITV actually passed up their option on the final and showed a film instead, but that was a morale-sapping (for their production team, at least) one-off.

Back to the 90s, and if I remember rightly, the BBC had taken the bullish view ahead of Italia '90 that having allowed ITV exclusively to show one of England's group games live, it wasn't going to relinquish any live England knockout games. ITV were welcome to do the same, and did so, but with England reaching the semis, that must undoubtedly have meant an advertising revenue hit. So, for France '98, when England had next qualified, the following division of matches had been agreed: the BBC would show England's opening game versus Tunisia and their final group game with Colombia. ITV would have just the second group game, against Romania, live, and in return would exclusively show an England second-round tie, if one arose. The BBC would then have a live England quarter-final to itself, and both channels would show any semi.

The expectation was that England would win their group, would then have a teatime second-round game with the runners-up in Argentina's group, and, all being well, a peak-time quarter-final and accompanying colossal audience. This seemed a reasonable gamble until England lost unexpectedly to Romania, finished second in their group and ended up with a peak-time second-round game against group winner and nemesis Argentina. This of course turned out to be an epic encounter which went to extra time and penalties – always a guarantee of exponential viewing figures – and peaked with 28 million people watching England go out of the competition on ITV. Not only was this comfortably the biggest audience of the tournament, it was one of the largest in modern television history. Well, of course it was, and it would have been the same figure if it had been presented by the Krankies live from a dungeon in Mongolia, but somehow it cast a bit of a shadow over proceedings, as if BBC Sport had dropped a terrible clanger. Two senior BBC executives, who shall remain nameless, came to Paris later in the tournament and seemed – to our general bewilderment – to regard this is a mortal blow to team morale, which it was their task to attempt to revive. They were also given our two complimentary tickets to the France v Croatia semi-final, amazing us all by reappearing at the studio before we were off the air. They'd left at half-time with France 1-0 down, before a Lilian Thuram-propelled comeback had sent the host nation into the final. I'm not sure whether or not wilfully missing that second half is a worse crime than Chris Evans tearing up those Euro '96 Final tickets, but neither grudge has abated, I'm afraid.

I thought this was all absolute nonsense, especially the obsession with ratings, but from the next football tournament onwards, by which time I was a programme editor and therefore quasi-management myself, I was to feel the same arbitrary pressures. We'd also lost Des and others by then, and in the course of the tournament were told that the primary reason for our continued existence had been snatched from us. The raison d'être of our fin de siècle a disparu, as they say in Paris.

5.

We'll be Back
after the Break

'We've lost *Match of the Day*.'

Andrew Clement and I, the two programme editors on site, had been asked to go into a quiet back room at the International Broadcast Centre in Amsterdam to have this alarming news broken to us five days into Euro 2000. Prior to setting off for the tournament, we'd been told a new rights deal was '99 per cent' in the bag, and that we were also about to regain the FA Cup and England rights. Instead, as I put it at the time, we'd won the icing and lost the cake: the FA deal had come off, but ITV had simultaneously outbid the BBC for the Premier League highlights package from 2001 to 2004.

I don't think I was alone in feeling physically sick. Niall Sloane, Gary Lineker and our live team in Brussels had the unenviable task of telling the audience we had lost the *Match of the Day* contract in the run-up to that evening's live game, Belgium v Italy. The next few days were not easy. It didn't help that our highlights studio and VT area in a Dutch conference centre were adjacent to ITV's so we could literally hear the champagne corks popping, and later that evening songs of triumph and mockery were heard outside our office door. I had, and have, several friends at ITV Sport so know that the witless gloating came from a minority, as it so often does from the glory-hunter breed of football fan. A few years later, I sent out a rare edict banning the use of that dreadful Americanism 'bragging rights' from *MOTD*.

That other American import 'suck it up, losers' sums up other reactions to the 'Snatch of the Day'. Ron Atkinson, co-commentating for ITV from a stadium position adjacent to the BBC team, decided that singing the *Match of the Day* theme at Barry Davies was a Wildean display of repartee, and ITV pundit Barry Venison (remember him?) spotted one of our young PAs, her job now in jeopardy, going through a security check and quipped, 'The BBC? Didn't you used to do football?'

Bad grammar, bad taste, bad haircut. Ray Stubbs, our highlights presenter in Amsterdam (that's football highlights, he wasn't Barry V's hairdresser), wanted to go round and punch his lights out. A noble enough reaction in the circumstances, but we were going to have to endure enough bad headlines as it was without Stubbsy getting arrested.

Sure enough, every newspaper went overboard the next day. One front page headline simply read 'The End'. At least we were out of the country as our obituary notices were being written and read. Brian Barwick, as head of ITV Sport, was understandably jubilant and cast himself as a latter-day Douglas Bader who had 'flown under the radar' to pull off an historic coup. We could have done without him subsequently suggesting that *MOTD* had been looking 'tired' and that ITV were going to 'shake it up'. In the end, they'd simply outbid us with heavier bags of swag, so the quality or otherwise of our programmes wasn't really the issue. 'Money doesn't talk, it swears,' as Bob Dylan once said. As the tournament wore on, a gallows humour swept the camp and, with great team players like Dion Dublin, Jamie Redknapp and Mick McCarthy on board, we actually had a thoroughly enjoyable trip. We had no idea what was going to happen to us professionally, but we were in a great city working on a classic tournament – Zidane's finest hour – so we were determined to enjoy it.

We'd shown the Netherlands v Italy semi live in Amsterdam. ITV had France v Portugal the next day in Brussels, so a group of us not involved with that night's highlights show rustled up a few media observer tickets, hired a car and drove down there. I'm glad we did. Zizou turned it on to a ridiculous degree – you'll still see many of his tricks and flicks from that evening whenever a Zidane montage is shown. It transpired that we were one observer seat short, so I ended up squeezing into the BBC commentary box alongside Motty, Lawro and their producer, my old *A Question of Sport* colleague Ken Burton. Thanks, guys. I also have particularly fond memories of stumbling out of a bar on to the canal side during that tournament, borrowing a busker's guitar and Messrs McCarthy and Dublin joining me and the production team in a booze-soaked and heartfelt rendition of Oasis's 'Don't Look Back in Anger'.

Reality set in once we got back home, but none of it turned out as badly as we'd feared. I put a lot of that down to one man: Greg Dyke. Greg had recently taken over as director-general of the BBC from John Birt, a rather remote figure whom *Private Eye* had always portrayed as a Dalek. Birt appeared to have little or no interest in sport; his only alleged contribution to the genre having been to express a preference for Barry over Motty as commentator for the 1994 World Cup Final. By contrast, Greg Dyke loved sport, especially football. Unlike his predecessor, whom I never met, he was a visible presence, turning up at our department meetings and events, and was a director at various times at Manchester United and Brentford FC before going on to chair the Football Association. The loss of *Match of the Day* on his watch had mortified him but instead of winding us down as we feared he might, he did the exact opposite. Firstly, he installed a high-profile TV figure in Peter Salmon as the newly designated director of BBC Sport. For the first time, sport was represented at the top table. Peter's CV included being a recent controller of BBC One, and although he was by no means a sports buff (and his strategy of concentrating our resources on a few big contracts upset some in the department), he did understand the value of football to the BBC[8].

There was a real danger after we lost the Premier League rights that our biggest names – Gary Lineker, Alan Hansen and John Motson – would be poached by our commercial rivals, so they were quickly given enhanced contracts. This may have led to issues in the later years of financial squeezes, but our football unit looked likely to fall apart at that point, so something had to be done. It was also decided from on high to recommission our weekly *Football Focus* and *Final Score* shows, despite the lack of Premier League footage. This made life far from easy for Andrew Clement's *Focus* team in particular, but the creative content required meant that we still needed a strong, year-round production team, and programme quality and viewing figures stayed remarkably buoyant.

We inevitably lost some commentators, pundits like Ally McCoist and three or four of our more experienced producers, to the expanding ITV Sport, but the guts were not ripped out of BBC Football as we'd feared. Niall was put in overall charge of football – managing the 'talent' and maintaining relationships with both the football authorities and the BBC hierarchy – and I replaced him as editor. It was a somewhat diminished role – for one thing, we only had one season of *Match of the Day* proper left on the Premier League contract – but I had no desire to recruit the main presenters or pundits, nor to haggle over their salaries, nor did I want to fight the big contractual and budgetary battles with the upper echelons of the corporation. Niall was much better at that kind of thing, as the following years were to prove. I was happy to make programmes and was left almost entirely free to do just that. Niall was always

8   Many years later, by now head of BBC North, Peter almost cost us Harry Redknapp as a *MOTD* studio guest in Salford one Saturday when he popped in to say hello and cheerfully told Harry that Spurs chairman Daniel Levy 'knows what he's doing' and 'doesn't suffer fools gladly'. Harry, who'd not long previously been sacked by Levy despite finishing fourth in the Premier League, wasn't happy.

available if we wanted to draw on his vast experience, and provided constructive feedback after the event, but he never interfered in running orders or anything else unless asked.

Even as football was being safeguarded, colleagues in the wider sports department were facing an uncertain future. There were ongoing battles about staffing levels and career prospects – I've just glanced back at a cache of emails from that era, and, my God, I was an angry shop steward pain in the backside about it all. The *Grandstand* team were badly affected by restructuring and contractual losses in the following decade, as were our technician friends and colleagues in the soon-to-be broken up and privatised BBC Resources. I was party to many heated meetings and email exchanges throughout this period, but others who found themselves directly in the eye of the storm would be better qualified to write that particular book.

That last highlights season with Gary went relatively smoothly, but as it wore on the question of how we'd sign off at the end of the final programme started to rear its head. Back in the autumn of 1999, after the previous barren season which had led to Des's departure, a one-off live European game had come the BBC's way. With Serbia off limits due to the conflict in Kosovo, Leeds United's away UEFA Cup tie with Partizan Belgrade had been moved to the Netherlands. I had edited *Football Focus* the previous weekend, and Ray Stubbs had the neat idea of using the commercial television phrase 'Back after the break' for our reappearance as a live football broadcaster. We hadn't used it in the end, because the game and circumstances didn't seem momentous enough, but I'd stored it away. I now thought it would fit in nicely somewhere during that last *MOTD* show, maybe in a VT trail for the non-Premier League goodies we still had available to us later in the year. As so often in our association, Gary took a half-baked, second-hand idea and made it into something memorable. 'We'll be back after the break,' were the last words spoken on a BBC Premier League highlights show for three years.

In the autumn of 2001, ITV launched *The Premiership*. We've established that I'm not a fan of bragging rights and gloating, so let's say straight away that the idea of mounting a highlights show at 7pm had also previously had considerable traction at the BBC. One of Des Lynam's justified complaints before leaving the BBC had been about *MOTD*'s increasingly erratic on-air times. More recent Premier League contracts insist that the show starts no later than 10.30pm, with the exception of *Festival of Remembrance*, *Last Night of the Proms* and *Eurovision Song Contest* nights, from memory. In Des's later years hosting the show, it was seen as a reliable and versatile filler in the schedule which could maintain a decent audience even if it slipped to 11pm. A fixed 7pm on-air time was mooted, but never happened. Also, an ITV production team can do nothing about commercial breaks, they're an existential fact of life – so an hour-long ITV highlights show will inevitably contain less match action than its BBC equivalent.

When the audience figures proved to be lower than those previously achieved by *Blind Date* in the same 7pm slot, and the statistics showed there was less football being shown than before, ITV and Des were hammered by the tabloids. I felt a bit for Des: he'd gone there as a fully-fledged 'national treasure' to host major live games and get away from the weekly grind, and now he was in the firing line and soon to find himself back at 10.30pm and beyond, more or less where he'd started, though presumably better paid. Even the much-maligned Tactics Truck was a relatively harmless alliterative gimmick which would have scarcely been noticed in other circumstances. That said, I always felt they missed a trick by not getting Tic-Tacs to sponsor it. Ironically, later in the decade, Tic-Tacs were to make an unscheduled appearance on ITV when their network control centre mistakenly ran in an advert for them during a live Everton v Liverpool FA Cup tie. To be fair, that's a cheap shot. We've all fallen off the air at some point, it was clearly beyond the productions team's control and missing a 118th-minute winning goal is every sports broadcaster's worst nightmare. I'm only mentioning it now, safe in the knowledge that it can no longer happen to me.

The net result of all of this (as unfair and arbitrary in its way as awards and the viewing figures circus) was that *Match of the Day* was considerably more popular in its absence than it ever had been when it was on the air. 'You don't know what you've got 'til it's gone', as Joni Mitchell sang about trees. We all kept a dignified public silence about the whole *The Premiership* affair – we knew these things tend to go in cycles. I did permit myself just one small moment of relatively private *Schadenfreude*. Our annual Christmas *MOTD* lunch, always held away from our workplace on an early December Monday, had traditionally been subsidised for staff, not all of whom were particularly well paid. Now, in a new era of financial restraints and transparency, everyone had to pay full price. I referred ruefully to this in my editor's speech, adding, 'but spare a thought for ITV. They've paid £180m for their turkey.' The BBC's racing correspondent, Cornelius Lysaght, included this line in a diary piece in *The Times*, but fortunately didn't name me. Sorry, ITV friends – yes, it was my line. For the most part, we'd moved on and just enjoyed making some lively shows of our own. We now had FA Cup and England home live games and some rights money left over to buy one-off away games and Liverpool and Celtic's runs to the 2001 and 2003 UEFA Cup Finals respectively. We even covered live Old Firm games for the whole UK for a while as part of BBC Scotland's SPL contract, which was both an eye-opener and great fun.

The biggest stroke of luck of all though came on 1 September 2001. Germany 1 England 5 in a World Cup qualifier in Munich. Motty picked it as his favourite game of his entire 50 years when he left the BBC in 2018, so it was genuine once-in-a-lifetime stuff for all of us in something like the eighth live game I'd ever edited or Phil Bigwood had ever studio directed. We'd brought in our top match director Alan Griffiths and our own crew to cover the game, and we broadcast *Football Focus* and *Grandstand* from Munich all day, which helped to justify taking our whole operation on the road. As Michael Owen scored his third goal of the game, and Motty yelled, 'This is getting better and better and better' – were the three 'betters' deliberate, Motty? If so, bravo – I popped my head out of the door of our truck just to savour the noise from the England fans.

Not long afterwards, I was at Upton Park with Motty when then England coach Sven-Goran Eriksson sneaked up to greet him with a chuckling, 'It's getting better and better and better.' I've followed some remarkable events from the car park outside in my career but none more enjoyable than that evening in Munich. It was only marred slightly when after a riotous and very late night celebrating as a team, Greg Dyke cheerily greeted us at the airport next morning with the news that he'd just arranged for a special recap programme to be added to the BBC One schedules that very evening. Instead of going home to sleep off the after-effects of excess adrenaline and steins of beer, we were off to Television Centre to put another live show together. We pretended to look pleased, but at least we knew our new boss was enthusiastic about our work and on our side.

One footnote – Germany 1 England 5 was nominated for a BAFTA early in 2002, losing to *Channel 4 Cricket*. It was a competent, clean programme, but how could you go wrong with a game like that? At least the BBC had actually directed the excellent match coverage, whereas the following year we were nominated for an England 1 Argentina 0 game where the majority of the show was actually provided by someone from ITV. John Watts, their number-one match director, had been seconded to the 2002 World Cup host broadcaster, and he and his team directed that game in Sapporo. If England had drawn or lost either of those games, we'd never have been nominated. If I'd had to make a speech, I would have thanked my colleagues, then either Michael Owen or David Beckham for making it possible. What did I tell you about awards?

That 2002 World Cup was a difficult event for us to cover for many reasons. Firstly, it was played umpteen time zones away across two countries, Japan and South Korea and, secondly, with the defections to ITV and with Niall Sloane having moved upstairs, we had only two editors with any programme experience at all available to work across the entire World Cup output. I was one of them but still fairly raw, and the other, fortunately, was (and is) my friend of 30 years' standing Andrew Clement (he's still there at the BBC in Salford bashing away one-fingered at his keyboard, chuntering to himself). It was just as well we got on since we had to rota ourselves to take charge of every broadcast from the first live game at around 7am to the peak-time highlights finishing something like 14 hours later. Phil Bigwood was our main studio director for the first time at a tournament, Kay Satterley had recently taken charge of the mammoth task of production managing the most complex operation imaginable, and Gary was presenting his first World Cup as lead presenter. We'd become competent live broadcasters of those one-off occasions, but the slog and pressure of the longest of all tournaments was something new for us all.

Fortunately, freed from programme duty, Niall was able to devote time to assembling a studio team. He was a thoroughly sociable guy who was happy to pursue a potential studio star like Leonardo for months after he saw him speak at a conference, with a view to getting him on board for the 2006 World Cup. He was also adept at dealing with the financial aspect; as I've already hinted, I managed to get through my entire BBC career without discussing the 'talent's' contracts, or ever even knowing what they were paid, but Niall enjoyed the cut and thrust of negotiations. As we've seen, he'd already recruited David Ginola and Martin O'Neill for France '98 – a masterstroke as it turned out – and for 2002, he'd lined up Peter Schmeichel, Ian Wright and Peter Reid to join Martin and Alan Hansen.

Niall's approach was uncannily similar to the one I later heard the great New Zealand cricket captain Brendon McCullum cite as applying across Kiwi international sport – 'No Wankers'. Clearly all the above pundits had sporting credibility, but they had to be able to get on with each other, treat those behind the camera with respect and be team players. This applied the whole time I was at BBC Sport, so a class act like Jürgen Klinsmann or Gianluca Vialli could guest and fit in seamlessly. There was the odd wobble – as mentioned, 'Diva Dave' had his moments at France '98 and later Clarence Seedorf, lovely guy though he was, sometimes had slightly starry tendencies. To be fair, so would I if I were him, though I may have stopped short of asking for fresh mango late one evening in Salford, an area not noted for its tropical fruit consumption. But they were all thoroughly decent people with good manners, and if they hadn't been, they wouldn't have been invited back. The biggest punditry headache ahead of 2002 was the well-publicised bust-up between Ian Wright and Peter Schmeichel a couple of years earlier on the pitch at Highbury. They were initially scheduled not to appear together, but after a chance meeting as they were checking in at the Kensington Hilton, they ended up chatting away all evening like long-lost brothers and asked to be paired together on air as soon as possible.

That story gives you some idea of what both men are like. Peter was the same gentle giant everyone loved when he appeared on *Strictly,* but he also had a steely side. Wrighty was complex: he wasn't yet quite the mature, relaxed pundit now regularly enhancing *Match of the Day* and *606,* but at his best he was always an amazing, uplifting presence in any company. We discovered in due course that everyone who'd shared a dressing room with him, including Arsene Wenger when they bumped into each other in a car park at Euro 2004, and even uncompromising opponents like Mick McCarthy, loved him. I first met him briefly when he made a one-off appearance on *MOTD* back in Des's day. 'This is my Graceland,' he said, as he stepped on to the hallowed set for the first time, and immediately had the entire production team on his side. The first time I took charge of a show on which he appeared was the crucial England v Greece qualifier at Old Trafford in October 2001. Niall was in the process of booking Wrighty for the subsequent World

Cup and wanted to give him a run out alongside Alan Hansen and Peter Reid ahead of finalising that booking.

For those big shows – we had something like two hours' build-up that Saturday afternoon – Gary Lineker and I had formed a habit we maintained for a decade and a half of getting together in advance over a coffee to write the script. Contrary to many people's assumptions, Gary comes up with the vast majority of his own words. He likes language, and even wrote his own column for the *Leicester Mercury* as a young player. I would plot out a running order, and maybe some guide words if I had a cunning plan for linking two apparently unrelated items, but Gary rightly wanted to use wording with which he was comfortable. He'd learnt 'less is more' watching Des and they both had an unerring instinct for removing an unnecessary line or finding a simpler way of saying something.

I had a specific line in mind for the start of the England v Greece show, though, and had run it past my colleague, Ian's ex-strike partner Mark Bright. Once he'd reassured me that Wrighty would love it, I gave it to Gary: 'Joining Alan Hansen, something most footballers can't do, Reid and Wright.' We kept it back until we went on air, and they all laughed, seemingly genuinely. Later, David Beckham scored that superb injury-time free kick to send England to the finals. It's become a bit of a cliché now, but the studio reaction shot we'd recorded was priceless, so we played it in after the extra angles of the goal. Because Becks scored so late in the game, the studio lights were up, the cameras were in go mode and the spontaneous celebrations, which culminated in Wrighty dancing on the desk, were impossible to resist, and caught the national mood, or certainly the mood in our vans where we'd all temporarily lost the plot, too.

Come the competition itself, we had another original idea which became commonplace. For the first BBC live England game versus Argentina, David Beckham's chance to atone for his 1998 red card against the same opponents, there was a daytime kick-off time in the UK. We asked each BBC region to send a camera to a factory, school or army barracks, to get shots of groups of fans watching our output. When Beckham – Goldenballs – once again played ball, and stuck his redemptive penalty away just before half-time, we had a sequence of gatherings of people nervously awaiting the kick, then going mad, across the country, which could hardly have worked out better if we'd planned it that way. And Wrighty was like a big kid – 'I love this! Just look at all that joy,' he shouted, temporarily co-presenting with Gary, which helped convince the powers-that-be that the whole thing was a stroke of genius.

Other than that highly enjoyable broadcast, I found the first phase of that World Cup as tough as anything I've ever worked on. ITV had an innovative double presentation approach – Des with the main pundits, the always excellent Gabby Logan (who was later to transfer in the opposite direction) with some well-chosen sofa guests, notably Ally McCoist who'd been on our books at France '98, as had several of his new senior production team. And much of the press, then as now, was itching to rubbish anything the BBC did or does. Until a set of head-to-head viewing figures came out after the first England knockout game with Denmark – Peter Salmon, our boss, had bullishly refused to concede any England knockout game exclusivity to ITV, just the one group game versus Sweden – we had no idea whether the usual ratings gap existed between us and ITV, and, as a new team, we were all on edge. And we were absolutely knackered with two live games most mornings, an evening highlights show and no rest days.

I was certainly feeling the pressure as an editor. Occasional live games and highlights shows since I'd become an editor were no real preparation for the incessant and remorseless burden of responsibility I was now encountering. Suddenly, everything felt like it was on my shoulders – Motty had been tickled by the idea that his commentaries in the afternoon or evening (his time) were being watched in the morning back at home. He began to inject his commentaries with boyish alliterative references to 'bacon with

Batistuta' and 'bagels with Beckham'. It really wasn't doing anyone any harm, but about a week in, I uncharacteristically asked him over talkback to stop it. And in the spirit of even-handedness, I then had a bit of a go at Barry Davies for his lack of sympathy with the Italians as they went out to a second-round extra-time golden goal against co-hosts South Korea. Back in London, we thought they'd been on the wrong end of some distinctly dodgy refereeing, notably a second yellow for their star player Francesco Totti, awarded for diving when he'd clearly done no such thing. A couple of incorrect offside calls and a highly debatable penalty award to their opponents had also gone against the Azzurri, but Barry still seemed to be holding a grudge against Italy from their ultra-defensive elimination, despite incurring two red cards, of the entertaining Dutch hosts at Euro 2000. He launched into a schoolmasterly broadside: 'The Italians never learn and now they have exactly what they deserve.' I thought they'd been really unlucky, and possibly diddled, and told Barry as much[9]. I'd scarcely ever felt I had the right to intervene in the commentaries of these two broadcasting titans before, other than if I felt something needed explaining to the viewers or a rare factual error had been made, so I was clearly feeling a little under the cosh.

England beating Denmark provided great relief for us on two fronts: the viewing-figure comparisons were the same as ever, if not better, and some of us were off to Japan. It had been agreed at stratospheric BBC levels that while it was logistically impossible to host the early part of the tournament from Asia, we could go on site if England made the quarter-finals. And just to add to the appeal, they were going to play Brazil. I'm not sure Andrew Clement has

---

9   Byron Moreno, referee in that Korea v Italy tie, was suspended for 20 games by the Ecuadorian FA the following autumn for 'serious timekeeping errors'. He'd signalled six minutes' injury time in a league game then played 13, during which time a 2-3 deficit became a 4-3 win for a leading Quito team. Moreno was running for election to Quito council at the time. In 2011 he was imprisoned for two and a half years by a New York court for smuggling heroin into the US. In retrospect, perhaps that was one of my better footballing calls …

ever entirely forgiven me for this, but he was the editor staying in London and I was the one going to Japan. To be fair, he'd already been there for what sounded like a less- pressurised filming trip to see Gary when he was playing for Grampus Eight, and eventually went on to edit the next two World Cup Finals. And he went to USA '94 when I didn't, come to think of it. And he still directs the FA Cup Final match coverage now, so it all worked out OK in the end.

Within hours of that England win, Gary, Alan Hansen, Peter Reid, Ian Wright and a small production team gathered at Heathrow, bound for Tokyo. I'd been struggling to get anywhere near enough sleep with the constant pressure and 5am UK starts, so that flight to Japan was glorious. We were straight on to a train into Tokyo and then caught a bullet train to a hotel near Shizuoka, host city for the England v Brazil game. Producer Ian Finch and I had been invited on a pre-tournament venue tour of South Korea, during which Ian had worked out the Korean element of our opening titles[10], but, other than Gary and Alan (who'd played in two World Club Championship Finals there with Liverpool), I don't think any of us had been to Japan before. Gary's spoken Japanese from his spell living there turned out to be invaluable, particularly in restaurants where, unless we had a translator with us, he was the only person who ever had a clue what was happening. We had a wooden hut booked at the ground, along with some rudimentary equipment, but had brought our graphics generators and other hardware from London. The bulkiness of this gear and the 'to the second' precision of Japanese train timetables turned the day into the equivalent of those strange team-building exercises corporate executives are sometimes sent on. I'll never forget the sight of a human chain, including three great ex-England footballers, throwing cases of

---

10 A side trip to Suwon, 'the toilet capital of the world', with a guided tour of supposedly the most ornate public conveniences on the planet, and a mayor who gave a half-hour simultaneously translated after-dinner speech about local toilet manufacturing followed by an interview opportunity in the gents, prompted one of our less-well-remembered Korean filmed features during the 2002 World Cup. Perhaps you had to be there ...

equipment into a carriage, and then flinging themselves and their luggage on board as the clock ticked down the seconds to departure.

It was a fantastic trip. The Japanese public loved the England team and anyone even vaguely associated with them. 'Beckham-Owen' was the only expression you needed to elicit a shy smile from pretty much anyone, and in particular Wrighty and Japan enjoyed a mutual love affair. He was a human whirlwind, refusing to tolerate anyone not assimilating themselves in the Japanese culture, buying a kimono suit to wear at the World Cup Final, acting as MC at a quite insane late-night karaoke session, eating anything put in front of him and corralling a group of us into a bizarre afternoon at a massage ceremony. This involved plunging into alternate freezing and boiling water and being thumped with twigs by a large and brutal bloke, if I remember correctly. And they'd politely asked Wrighty to cover up the tattoo on his arm, which we later discovered was regarded as evidence of membership of a Yakuza criminal gang.

England were duly knocked out, but we stayed on for Brazil's semi-final with Turkey and their final against Germany. The night before the final, the whole BBC team went out to an al fresco restaurant at Yokohama harbour, which was positioned under the main landmark there, the world's biggest digital clock. Every hour on the hour, this clock exploded into life with digital fireworks in dazzling colours and a blast of cheesy music. Wrighty was very taken with this, and as the meal drew to a close, he began to wonder aloud what delights awaited when it chimed midnight in a few minutes' time. He decided that a team photo was in order and appointed himself David Bailey. Having arranged us where he wanted us, he decided that more people were required and started to herd all the waiters into the photo. Still not satisfied, he went indoors and re-emerged followed by a smiling crocodile of front-of-house management and all the chefs. I have no idea whether any actual photos materialised but it definitely allayed any pre-match nerves.

My final memories of that trip again involve Wrighty. The morning after Brazil lifted the trophy we took two trains to get to the airport through the Tokyo rush hour. Motty was standing on a platform and doubtless was still in the zone, reliving a big live commentary.

Ian Finch had been videoing various elements of our trip and Wrighty motioned him over and delivered a David Attenborough-style whispering piece to camera: 'Here we have the rare commentatorius intensitus ...' This went on for a couple of minutes before Motty twigged and joined in. Finally, as we were pulling into Narita station, someone said that the net total, not average, lateness for one of the bullet train routes in a year was something like 25 seconds. Wrighty, like all of us, had been bowled over by all things Japanese, but decided to test this out. We were due at Narita at 10.19am. As we pulled into the platform, he looked up at the station clock numbering the seconds. Sure enough, '10.18.55 ... 56 ...' and at the exact moment the doors opened, it clicked to '10.19.00'. Wrighty leapt off the train and sank to his knees as hundreds of bewildered commuters swarmed around, bawling, 'You people don't know how lucky you are to live in this country!'

When I think that several high-profile footballers on a coach trip to the Great Wall of China chose to stay on the bus playing cards (seriously), Wrighty's enthusiasm and fascination with unfamiliar surroundings helped turn a daunting trip into one we will all remember with a huge smile. We tried, wherever the pressures allowed, to take that attitude away with us throughout the years to follow.

Our tournament coverage went from strength to strength over the next decade or so. Apparently, though, I have to confess I didn't see all that much of it, so did ITV's in the same period – not surprising considering that by 2014, their entire senior production team (even Niall was there by then) as well as commentators Clive Tyldesley, Peter Drury and Jon Champion, presenter Adrian Chiles and his panel for the World Cup Final – Lee Dixon, Ian Wright and Niall's old mate Martin O'Neill – had been lured away from the BBC. Every tournament during this period saw the whole BBC team transplanted for the duration to a great city in the host nation. That is, with the exception of Euro 2012 where the geographically awkward split between co-hosts Poland and Ukraine meant we only went out there from the semis onwards. Incidentally, as a lifelong connoisseur of brutal post-industrial landscapes – I actually enjoy the walk from Middlesbrough station to the Riverside, thank you very much – I found Donetsk fascinating, and am drinking a coffee from my Cyrillic script Shakhtar mug as I type this sentence.

The next three World Cups (four, if you include Moscow after I left) were presented by Gary from a succession of conventionally glorious locations, with the Brandenberg Gate, Table Mountain and Copacabana Beach behind him, respectively. The studio guests became increasingly cosmopolitan, as had the Premier League and wider British society. Marcel Desailly, Clarence Seedorf, Jürgen Klinsmann, Gianluca Vialli, Rio Ferdinand, Thierry Henry – if you add in Schmeichel, Gullit, Ginola and a couple of the regular in-house guys (Alan Shearer, for one, was a regular by now), that's a World XI to take on all comers. All were impressive people and fascinating company as well as unimpeachably credible football pundits.

We also stepped up our feature-making in some historically extraordinary locations. Niall Sloane, Andrew Clement and I all saw football as the 'most important of all the unimportant things in life', as did Gary, so we tried to inject context into our programme output with extended features about Hitler's Berlin Olympics, the Holocaust memorial and the Berlin Wall through to the Battle of the Spion Kop and its Merseyside connections, the history of apartheid and Brazil's chequered path to racial equality and wonderful, creative culture against the backdrop of continuing social problems. We asked the superb creative producer, Chris Grubb, to devise and co-ordinate these films in due course, and often involved our own reporters: Adrian Chiles made some remarkable pieces in Berlin,

Garth Crooks made a fine hard-hitting film around the anniversary of the Soweto massacre, while Dan Walker and his namesake Rob toured South Africa in a BBC bus covering all manner of historical and current topics, and Jason Mohammad roamed far and wide to get under the cultural and musical skin of modern Brazil.

On other occasions, we involved our on-screen guests – the extraordinarily well-connected Clarence Seedorf interviewed Archbishop Desmond Tutu and some of the great football figures he knew, and Rio Ferdinand launched himself into our host city, especially its favelas, in 2014 to such an extent that it spawned a whole BBC One documentary, *Rio in Rio*. And Gary could also get out and about and pre-record tournament or big match opening sequences from the 1936 Olympic Stadium, up Table Mountain or at the Christ the Redeemer statue. Towards the end of the World Cup in 2010, Jürgen Klinsmann asked if he could have a copy of all the features our team had made in South Africa so he could take them home to show his kids. Like his fellow Jürgen, the charismatic Liverpool coach Klopp, Jürgen is a highly intelligent, socially aware representative of modern Germany, so the whole team regarded that as a massive compliment.

There were occasional mutterings from certain quarters, often rival media organisations, about the licence fee being spent taking our coverage to those tournaments, but in reality the bulk of the cost to the BBC went on the initial rights fee, satellite feeds and so on. The immediacy and visual impact of being on site, as well as the access to extra footage coming into the broadcast centre from the matches or from our international broadcasting colleagues, cost at most a few pence per viewer from their annual licence fee. At a time when the BBC was often under assault at home, our name still opened doors around the world. The biblical phrase 'a prophet is without honour in his own land' sprang to mind in my more pompous moments.

The BBC's name still attracted respect and admiration abroad when I made my last overseas trip, to Rio, and I'm sure it still does for the current generation who travel on Auntie's behalf. At Euro 2012, I walked down a corridor full of broadcasters at the brand-new National Stadium in Warsaw with Gary Lineker and Alan Shearer. Executive boxes had been converted by UEFA into temporary studios, all of which had been hired by various European national broadcasters for the Italy v Germany semi-final. We had Jürgen Klinsmann and Gianluca Vialli in tow as we arrived at our studio – a well-balanced and almost embarrassing array of talent. Four of the greatest international strikers of modern times: one German, one Italian and two English. The production team from TVP in Poland, and others, thought this was a magnificent line-up – as indeed it was, when you thought about it – and asked if they could pop in to ask a few pre-match questions of them. This happened frequently when we were on the road – as was generally the case, we took it as the compliment it was, and our four gents readily agreed.

The BBC was, and still is, almost universally admired around the world as a trusted broadcaster of record – whether you read the memoirs of Anne Frank or Mikhail Gorbachev, almost anyone living through troubled times, or under totalitarian regimes and unable to trust local propaganda, has tended to try to seek out the BBC for impartial, unimpeachable information. And in less straitened circumstances, everything from David Attenborough's wildlife programmes to *Dr Who* to the BBC Drama serialisation of *War and Peace* is watched around the globe and generally seen as a yardstick of quality.

The British public understandably has more mixed feelings. It doesn't help that almost all of our newspapers and some politicians bitterly resent the BBC's presence and would like it removed from the playing field, but beyond that the licence fee is an anachronistic method of taxation. Other than pensioners, the less well-off are discriminated against in real terms in that every address with a television set has to pay £150 a year for the BBC's services. No matter how often you point out that 41p a day per household won't buy you the *Daily Mail* or a packet of mints and isn't bad value for the whole of BBC television, radio and online – personally, even having left the place, I'd pay that just for *Desert Island Discs, Cunk on Britain* or *Blue Planet* – some people baulk at being asked to pay anything.

I never said, or say, where I work/worked without being asked, but have still been harangued for it by total strangers. My wife and I once shared a table on holiday with an elderly American lady who, having asked where I worked, gushed at length about her favourite BBC period dramas and comedies. A man from Devon sitting nearby with his wife overheard this and cheerfully announced that they hated the BBC, only ever watched Sky and didn't pay the licence fee. This was way back before Sky Atlantic had started to compete at the quality end of the market, and it turned out they weren't even sports fans. When he subsequently revealed that he ran a Toyota dealership, I was sorely tempted to trash his job like he just had mine, but what would have been the point? Especially as I know very little about cars.

The tipping point in the corporation's 21st-century fortunes had come for many of us back in 2004 when our enormously popular director-general Greg Dyke had felt obliged to resign after the publication of the Hutton Report, which had severely criticised the BBC's coverage of the build-up to the Iraq War and – remarkably – pretty much exonerated Tony Blair's government. I never bought into BBC Sport's subsequent chumminess with Alastair Campbell and once shouted across at him at half-time in a Boro game at Turf Moor that Burnley were '45 minutes from doom'. Rather like the search for WMDs, the match in fact ended 0-0.

The BBC as a whole has recovered reasonably well from that troubled period in its history, arguably better than British politics has, but the biggest ongoing sticking point in many people's relationship with it, and the area in which the corporation is still under most scrutiny, is news. The 'we're always on last' charge is a pain when you're editing *Match of the Day,* but similar accusations of bias in the news arena are frequently toxic, and it's more difficult than ever to achieve balance and meaningful scrutiny in the current era of spin, politicians appealing to emotion rather than reason and charges of fake news. I'm so glad that my politics-based degree didn't come into play and that I spent my career working on the joyous diversion that is sport. 'Stick to football', as Gary Lineker is told by certain people every time he mentions anything else on Twitter, and move on to a new chapter.

6.

Auntie Social

No one at the BBC is ever allowed to forget that they are employed by the public, or at least the law-abiding ones who pay their licence fee. Audience feedback and increasingly participation go with the territory, particularly when you take charge of programmes watched by millions.

When I joined the BBC in the late 80s, and for a decade or so afterwards, there were three main ways for a viewer to make their opinions known to a programme maker: a phone call, a letter, or by knowing or meeting someone who worked on the programme. If you were in the industry, you could also carp directly or indirectly, sometimes to some effect. One of my first chances to edit a match for *Match of the Day* was an FA Cup tie in the early 90s. It was a gutsy, against the run of play, giant-killing performance by a Third Division side against top-flight opposition. Instead of basking in the afterglow, the winning manager – let's call him Colin – singled out *MOTD* in his local press for producing an edit allegedly biased against his team. Our studio producer, Vivien Kent, got wind of this accusation, and, not unreasonably, asked me about it. I dug out my log of the game and took it into Viv's office. Although Colin's team had played out of their skins in a hanging-on-for-grim-death way, their opponents had almost all the best chances in the game but either missed them or were foiled by the keeper. Inevitably, this is what a relatively short edit is mostly going to feature. Fortunately, I wasn't taken off match-editing duty, nor have I held a grudge against 'one of the game's characters' for the last quarter of a century ...

But back to complaints from the public. Phone calls were logged by the wonderfully named Duty Office – what a great, public service-inspired name it sounds, though it only really meant the poor sod on phone duty when, say, *Match of the Day* was live on the air – and passed on to the editor of the programme. A significant volume of calls on any contentious subject and you'd be expected to reply. 'I didn't like Des Lynam's tie tonight' would be passed on, but you didn't have to do anything about it. I don't think there were any rules about letters, but if someone had taken the trouble to put pen to paper it was felt by our department that they should get a reply.

As I was later to discover as editor, most of the correspondence to *Match of the Day* was as one-eyed as Colin the manager: supporters of team A swearing blind that the programme was wildly biased against them and conducting a love affair with their local rivals, team B. As a multi-sports programme, *Grandstand*'s post bag had mostly consisted of aficionados of various sports failing to see the overall editorial picture. It must seem bizarre to a younger generation brought up on sports channels, but back then the editor of *Grandstand* was effectively a man with a zapper deciding when to leave a Test match to go to the big race at Haydock and how quickly to return afterwards ('here are the wickets which have fallen since we've been away from Lord's') and how best to fit in live or recorded snooker, motor sport or whatever else was billed. There was no second channel, red button or online streams to get you out of jail, as there are now at Wimbledon or the Olympics. If the contract said you had to show the 2.15 from Newbury, you had to leave the cricket at a suitable, or often not suitable, juncture. It was a difficult juggling act, as I was to discover when occasionally let loose on it further down the line.

Most people accepted these long-established parameters, or at least just groaned in their living rooms, but furious letters would still appear the following week: 'Sir, at 2.59 on Saturday afternoon, you chose to leave a beautifully poised Test match with Gooch and Gower at the crease for some ghastly horse race,' vs 'Sir, your appalling decision to abort your interminable cricket coverage at the last possible moment cost me the chance to see Winalot Boy in the paddock before the 3.00 at Ascot and ruined the coverage for me and my family.' Confronted with this kind of impossible conundrum every week for years, the great maverick *Grandstand* editor John Philips is alleged to have, on occasion, simply sent cricket man the racing letter and vice versa. I hope he did. In the current climate of social media, demands for accountability, complaints units and rigid procedures, you'd probably be sacked for even thinking of doing that, but it made the point about occasionally seeing the argument from both sides.

Then there were the clashes between the sports and non-sports audiences. Many licence-payers resent the disruption a sporting event can cause to the regular schedules. If live sport was ever delayed or overran and caused, say, *Gardeners' World* or *Antiques Roadshow* to start after the billed time or – God forbid – to be cancelled altogether, the number of complaints could reach treble or even quadruple figures. There are many advantages to working on a big sporting occasion for the BBC: massive free-to-air audiences; no adverts to interrupt the flow or send viewers to the other channel during a head-to-head World Cup Final; the resources to cover it properly (budget cuts permitting); cross-promotion and input from other parts of the organisation and backing from on high within the organisation. Even director generals and channel controllers with no personal interest in 'muddied oafs and flannelled fools' (bit of Kipling there, ladies and gentlemen) know that the public consistently place major sporting events near the top of any list of their licence fee expectations. However, there are times when, as a programme editor, you envy your Sky counterparts working for umpteen channels only showing sport, and where you presumably don't have to explain extra time and penalties in the middle of a classic FA Cup Final to someone who's hellbent on taking you off the air to show *Doctor Who*. Let me explain.

May 2006 saw the last of six FA Cup Finals to be held in Cardiff while Wembley was being redeveloped. Great ground though it was and is[11], none of our live finals held in Wales had really caught fire. Until this one, that is. Underdogs West Ham raced into a two-goal lead, Liverpool pegged them back to 2-2, then fell behind again. Deep into injury time, Steven Gerrard produced one of the great FA Cup Final moments of any era with a cartoon-like blooter – or thronker, if you're Dan Walker – from outside the box. By now, I'd been editing live football for a few years and we all knew that, out of courtesy, the production co-ordinator in charge of our programme would press a talkback button and let the network know that extra time was looming. We'd had a few of these situations in tournaments and knockout matches – not least our previous final involving Liverpool in the 2001 UEFA Cup – and the protocol was a one-line 'Understood' over talkback and a chat on the phone once extra time was underway about likely new off-air times. This time, with the full-time whistle about to blow and our entire team needing to know the hastily revised sequence of analysis we'd be using to fill the gap while tired on-field legs were massaged, the batphone connecting our van in Cardiff to BBC One network control in London rang. A voice on the other end started to witter on about *Doctor Who*, at which point the final whistle went. I bluntly told him that we'd have to speak again during extra time and hung up just in time to talk everyone through five minutes of improvised live television ahead of the restart.

Just to put what followed into perspective, I should say that 99 per cent of my dealings with network control over the years

---

11 As a Boro fan, our finest-ever hour came there in the League Cup Final of 2004. A first major trophy in our 128-year history after repeated Wembley misery.

were smoothness personified. I realised early on that they had an unenviable macro version of my job – trying to make a whole day and evening's shows of every shape and size fit into a complex schedule – and keeping them in the loop would be wise, not least when there was a chance we'd need a favour from them. I made a point of calling them in advance of any live show to discuss what might happen. Not surprisingly, given that they are asked to be such all-rounders, some of them understood sport completely and were already ahead of us, others less so. We'd occasionally ask for an extra 30 seconds or minute to fit everything we'd edited into a particularly packed Saturday night *Match of the Day*. Sometimes we'd get it, sometimes we wouldn't. Our well-mannered PA Anne Somerset was once refused an extra 30 seconds on my behalf on a particularly manic Wednesday night on the grounds that some viewers would have pre-set their videos to record the *Deaf Zone* which followed us at 00.10am. Anne claims that my reply on talkback to this was an incredulous 'F--- the f---ing *Deaf Zone*,' but I'm sure she misheard me. I do recall snapping, 'We're just the meat in your sandwich, aren't we?' when an overly long *EastEnders* omnibus lopped off some of our transmission time for a Weymouth v Bury Sunday afternoon cup extravaganza, but I was uncharacteristically tired and tetchy that day. I generally got on well with the network controllers and understood their situation. Most of the time.

Back to Cardiff. One of those socks-round-the-ankles periods of extra time was unfolding on the monitor in front us, as I called network control back to try to make sense of this *Doctor Who* gibberish. 'This is a nightmare,' said the voice at the other end who shall remain nameless, not least because he was behaving like a dick. 'We've got to get to *Doctor Who* on time.'

We knew the news was following us, then there was a *Strictly* spin-off, with *Doctor Who* scheduled after that at 7pm. I like to think I have a sense of where sport belongs in the scheme of things – that 'most important of all the unimportant things in life' – and I'd always understood news's pre-eminence. We would happily, as always, put up a caption and get John Motson to remind viewers that the news would follow us, we'd bust a gut after live midweek games to hit the *Ten O'clock News* on time, we'd accommodate any newsflash they called for, and had even switched channels when world events dictated. On this occasion, though, it was a humdinger of an FA Cup Final, and unless something really major was happening in the wider world, Motty's line to his producer when asked to wrap the Italy v Brazil World Cup classic of 1982 sprang to mind: 'But this *is* the news.' In any case, the news bulletin wasn't the problem: our man was obsessed with *Doctor Who* and its 7pm slot.

'How long is this going to last?' was the first demand.

There had been international experiments with Golden and Silver Goals during this era, so I was patient:

'Thirty minutes, plus injury time,' I replied.

'Jesus Christ.'

I paused before gently lobbing the next grenade:

'And, of course, if it's still a draw at the end of that, it goes to penalties.'

'Penalties? How long will that take?'

'Well, there'll be a pause and then it depends whether it finishes 4-2 or 17-16.'

'That's ridiculous. I need to know what time *Doctor Who* will get on.'

This was now so surreal, and distracting, that I actually didn't lose my temper. I just said we'd speak later, and in something of a trance by now, summed up the conversation for Gary and the guys in the studio, who'd heard my end of it over our talkback. They were stunned, but studio director Phil Bigwood and I were united in saying simply that we'd win our case and argue the toss on Monday.

I thought our mate in network control would eventually realise that, though we sympathised, events had now taken charge and there wasn't much we could do. Even so, I found myself hoping someone would score a winner to take the sting out of this bizarre stand-off. Instead, with a few minutes to go in extra time and neither exhausted team having made a breakthrough, there was another call. I'm paraphrasing, but all present at our end would vouch for the gist of this:

'This is going to penalties, isn't it?' (accusing tone)

'Looks like it.'

'Right, as soon as someone wins, you have to get off the air.'

'Er, the trophy presentation?'

'Nope, no time for that.'

I paused, truly lost for words, and eventually came up with:

'I wouldn't do that if I were you. If you do, you'll lose your job.'

He hung up again. We were incredulous – we'd been on the air since 1pm and not only were closing titles and interviews about to be sacrificed, they were intent on missing the trophy being lifted, presumably for the first time since the FA Cup Final was first televised by the BBC in the 1930s.

There wasn't time for us to refer this up the chain within BBC Sport, so Phil and I resolved that we would do something neither of us had ever done before, refuse to wrap up the show early, and defy BBC One to take us off the air at their own peril. We didn't know whether this would constitute a court-martialling offence but were pretty sure that our immediate bosses would back us up after the event. Whether we'd have been as sure of our ground when we were less experienced a few years earlier is another matter. Even so, it was all a bit terrifying. And all for a *Doctor Who* episode that was presumably timeless. In the sense that, unlike our show, it was recorded and could go out anytime if necessary, and also because, well, he was the Time Lord, wasn't he?

Fortunately, the ever-resourceful, never booked in his career, supremely well-connected Gary Lineker, listening in to this nonsense, had quietly texted the extremely capable BBC One controller Peter Fincham. Just as we were waiting for the penalties to start, and preparing for mutiny, we had yet another call from network control. It was as if a different person had taken charge – think Peter Capaldi morphing into Jodie Whittaker – and we were told in honeyed tones to make sure we didn't come off air until we'd interviewed the main protagonists, followed by a polite inquiry as to how long our closing montage was going to be. I like to picture Peter Fincham's hand coming out of the end of an old-fashioned telephone and giving his network editor's nose a yank, in the style of Dick Dastardly's general. That would have been richly deserved. And of course, both the football and the delayed *Doctor Who* transmission pulled in enormous audiences. Whatever had happened, suffice to say, nothing like that ever happened to us again. Which was good news for what remained of my hair. [12]

My arrival as a permanent programme editor in 2000 had coincided with the early days of widespread email and internet, so we were encouraged to get the audience involved. Euro 2000 had been one of the launch pads for this brave new mission into cyberspace, and, on the highlights show in particular, we loudly trumpeted that we were looking for contributions from 'you at home'. Based on a ropey *Guys and Dolls*-related pun, 'Zidane, you're rocking the boat', which hadn't found an outlet at France '98, we asked the public to come up with Euro 2000-related song titles. These days, Dan Walker has only to tweet #tvshowXI for some wag to fire back 'Downton Xavi' or 'Quedrue Do You Think You Are?' within seconds; back in those analogue times, almost no one participated. Only the production team seemed interested. Actually, it was me masquerading as my wife ('Amanda from Stockton') and that era's editor of *Grandstand*, and fellow fan of dodgy wordplay, 'Carl from Widnes' (of Atlanta 'Nice Day Nazi' rage fame) in his armchair at home, who provided 90 per cent of them. We ploughed on for a few days, but other than Carl's Anglo-German effort 'Khan

12 With the help of Genome, my exhaustive research has unearthed the planned *Radio Times* schedule for BBC One that FA Cup Final evening: 1740 *BBC News*; 1800 *Strictly Dance Fever*; 1900 *Doctor Who* (Rise of the Cybermen Part One, no less). The evening's viewing concluded, perhaps appropriately, at 0020 with *Morons from Outer Space*.

Barmby Love' whose ingenuity I happen to remember, it's all sadly lost to posterity.

Compared to some of the other antics going on across the BBC and the whole TV industry – dodgy competitions, fake interviewees, the secret renaming of a *Blue Peter* cat – our mild sleight of hand was small beer, but along with *Football Focus* 'viewers' questions' which had sometimes been spiced up with better ones from the production team, it subsequently all had to be disclosed in an exhaustive BBC inquiry. There had been too much pressure put on some production teams to be interactive and audience-friendly to the point where if there weren't any calls or correct competition entries, no one dared admit it and varying levels of deception had sometimes crept in.

I was volunteered as a 'Safeguarding Trust' champion, which meant I had to conduct seminars using some of the worst broadcast examples: radio hosts interviewing 'competition winners' who were actually members of the production team phoning in from the room next door; a notorious trailer that edited the Queen hurrying into a room so it looked like she was 'storming out', and the rest of it. Every single person who worked at the BBC had to sit, cringing, through about an hour of this, and I was charged with getting the sports department 'talent' up to speed. The pugnacious rugby pundit and lawyer Brian Moore asked some forensically challenging questions, whereas a bizarre pre-*Match of the Day* Saturday lunchtime session with Lineker, Shearer and Hansen brought the *Beano*'s Bash Street Kids to mind. I don't think any of them had been in a classroom situation in decades, and I'm not sure how much trust we safeguarded, but we got through it, and we were duly trusted enough to be allowed to bring Goal of the Month and Season back, albeit with all manner of elaborate safeguards. That only went awry a few years later when the public were allowed to vote ...

These days, you can conduct whole segments of radio shows from genuine texts and tweets from the public, and whole shows

Rehearsal: author with Gary Lineker in BBC Euro 2008 studio, Vienna. (Photo courtesy of Tony Bate)

MOTD production office, 2007. Alan Shearer, Gary Lineker and me with director Jim Irving as Ringo. (Photo courtesy of Mary McCartney/ Macmillan Cancer Charity)

A Question of Sport – the classic late 1980s Coleman-Beaumont-Hughes line-up whose production team I joined. On this occasion, Princess Anne was amongst the guests.

Two of the 1988 A Question of Sport production team – Ray Stubbs, in his pre-presenter/reporter days, and me.

MOTD welcomes Pele for the 1995 Umbro Cup, and pre-selfie mania breaks out. Left to right: Stuart Cabb, Pele, Asmi Ahmad, me.

Filming **The Essential FA Cup Final**, *1997: with interviewer Mark Demuth, Sir Stanley Matthews and cameraman Jon Lord.*

Moscow, April 1998: Snow meets undersoil heating overkill. Standing in front of the burnt surface on which Spartak were about to play Inter in a UEFA Cup semi-final.

The BBC World Cup on-air six-a-side team for France 1998. Hill, Davies, Motson, Hansen, Lynam, Lineker.

After a marathon 18-hour overnight journey from Shepherd's Bush, the author and Alan Hansen arrive at Shizuoka for England v Brazil, June 2002 (video stills courtesy of Ian Finch).

The photo which adorned my much-missed BBC Sport blog. And still Boro fans contacted me to say they were 'always on last'.

The BBC production team on the studio balcony overlooking the Place de la Concorde, France '98. I'm in sunglasses, fellow editor Andrew Clement is far left, Albert Sewell and Niall Sloane are just behind the replica trophy.

With director Ian Finch and vision mixer Dave Fitzpatrick as we produce the BBC's World Cup coverage from a portacabin in a car park outside the stadium in Yokohama, July 2002 (video still courtesy of Ian Finch)

Cardiff, 29 February 2004. Three generations of both sides of the family gather to see the end of a 128-year Middlesbrough trophy drought.

The greatest single moment in the history of football. Massimo Maccarone completes a second Boro four-goal comeback in three weeks. Middlesbrough v Steaua Bucharest, UEFA Cup semi-final, 2006

Berlin 2006. Table football in the BBC production office (left to right) – me, Ian Wright, Leonardo, BBC producer Pete Andrews (Photo courtesy of Melisa Cregeen)

Two legends of the visual arts, plus Alan Hansen. Spike Lee drowns his sorrows at our post-World Cup Final drinks in a Berlin bar. And yes, deckchair shirts were all the rage back in 2006. (Photo courtesy of Melisa Cregeen)

Vienna, 2008 – with the presenter during Euro 2008 studio rehearsal (Photograph courtesy of Tony Bate).

Uganda 2007. Sport Relief trip with BBC Sport, group photo after an arduous football match with the local kids. Even Les Ferdinand looks like he's been given the runaround. (Photograph courtesy of Comic Relief)

Cape Town World Cup 2010 studio team – Dixon, Shearer, Hansen and Lineker – watch a live game and prepare to demand some fiendish analysis for half-time. (Photo courtesy of Jim Cullen)

Brazil 2014. A BBC World Cup team meal, sitting between Dan Walker and Kevin Kilbane (photo courtesy of Jo Tranmer)

My first World Cup not working for the BBC since this man won a Golden Boot in 1986. BBC Sport studio, Red Square, Moscow, June 2018.

(and not just at 2am) from their phone calls. I say you can, but if you'll forgive me, I may well not be listening if you do. I have some sympathy with John Motson who, faced with some call to arms or other to deliver in commentary pleading for viewer participation, once asked, exasperated, in a meeting: 'Who's broadcasting to who here?' Technically, it should have been 'whom', Motty, but it was a point well made. By contrast, Michael Gove's pre-EU referendum claim that we've 'had enough of experts', while reflecting the zeitgeist pretty accurately was, to my mind, a dreadful thing for any politician – or broadcaster – to say. Whether sport, economics or my medical welfare are being discussed, I want to hear from qualified people who know something about the subject at hand, not from the nearest pub bore. To quote a friend of mine, I don't even care all that much what I think about football, so I certainly don't want to hear from Dave from Cornwall who supports Manchester United, didn't go today (or ever), but is convinced from the message boards that the referee was a City fan, the players didn't show enough passion and that 'he has to go'. The manager, that is, not Dave. Dave's going nowhere, unfortunately.

To be fair, there are many situations where you would want to hear from eye-witnesses or those directly affected by a government policy, and it is possible for a talented host to conduct a listenable phone-in. James O'Brien manages to do just that most days on LBC and Danny Baker's original 606 on BBC 5 Live was often superb, largely because asking for tales of animals holding up play, or the most ridiculous thing you've been allowed to take into a football ground – a chef finishing a shift and realising he had all his kitchen knives with him as he entered the turnstiles, if I recall correctly – and some judicious vetting by the production team made for genuinely interesting and funny calls from fans of clubs of all sizes.

By contrast, I couldn't stand David Mellor's subsequent humourless and big club dominated incarnation of 'red-hot soccer chat'. Old-school, proper Chelsea fan Andrew Clement – in a rare display of the kind of wit his father Dick used to display as co-writer of *The Likely Lads* and *Porridge* – was heard to chunter back then that the show was called *606* because it was impossible to last more than six minutes and six seconds without smashing up your radio. It's somewhat better these days in that the presenter tends to be well informed and sits alongside someone with genuine football credibility. Kelly Cates is an excellent foil for Ian Wright, for example, and even if the occasional over-entitled, glory-seeking caller sets my teeth on edge, they're usually gently put straight. And no one says 'red-hot soccer chat' any more.

I also disagreed loudly with putting Goal of the Month and Goal of the Season to a public vote. Though many people will be objective, the outcome's likely to end up skewed towards goals scored by the big clubs. You can also become the victim of a social media campaign. The tradition for the Goal of the Season shortlist was to include every Goal of the Month winner while leaving space for an entry from May in case something incredible occurred on the last day. So, when Jack Wilshere scored a decent volley v West Brom on the last day of the 2014/15 season, in it went. It was clearly not as good as Charlie Adam's preposterous goal for Stoke from his own half at Stamford Bridge, a ridiculous outside-of-the-foot lob from QPR's Bobby Zamora at West Brom, or most of the others. However, the Arsenal message boards and Twitter accounts went into overdrive, Wilshere won for the second season running (the previous one deservedly) and a somewhat embarrassed Lineker and Shearer had to politely agree to disagree. The public participation element changed after that to merely selecting a shortlist of three, allowing the pundits to make the final choice, but dinosaur-like, I thought, as I usually did, that democracy had gone too far.

For what it's worth, and to be consistent in my misanthropy, I also wasn't wild as an armchair viewer about the constant plugging of player ratings in the BBC's otherwise superb coverage of the 2018 World Cup. Whether the UK viewing public thought Saudi Arabia's left-back had earned a five or six out of ten against Egypt doesn't matter greatly. On the other hand, the persistent marking down of England's Raheem Sterling by people who either don't understand football or have swallowed a tabloid agenda about his wealth, tattoos or willingness to leave Liverpool was not pleasant to behold. It only takes the occasional malicious nought or one amongst the sincere appraisals to drag someone's average down below his team-mates. If Sterling really was England's worst player for game after game, then BBC pundits like Rio Ferdinand, Alan Shearer and Jürgen Klinsmann, who consistently praised his performances, must have been watching a different tournament. At least the on-air team very sensibly avoided referring to the ratings results.

Back when the concept of interactivity was in its infancy, I did have various stabs at becoming more social media friendly as *MOTD* editor. I was happy to contribute when Roger Mosey, then head of BBC Sport, introduced the concept of editors' blogs. Dozens of them are still online, if your life is lacking a certain something. For quite a while, I filed something most weeks or even every few days during a major event like the 2006 World Cup. I even felt a lot of love from the host nation after I wrote a piece entitled 'Frings ain't what they used to be' about being won over by Klinsmann and co after a lifetime of disliking the German national team, and by the wonderful experience of broadcasting from Berlin. By this stage, the Duty Office (renamed the Complaints Unit) filed emails and calls, so you'd get quite a bit of feedback after most shows, with many reasonable and answerable points cropping up.

I wrote blogs on the rationale behind a given running order, or an explanation of how we put the analysis together. See chapter seven 'Any Given Saturday' and remember – 'we want to hear from you'. Hang on, this is a book, that won't work. Or people would ask for longer match edits on the red button, and I'd explain how the contract didn't permit it. I was a bit constrained by where I worked, so had to politely argue our case, or agree that, yes, the scheduling wasn't ideal, or, yes, it's a shame we've just lost the FA Cup contract again[13], but answering viewers' queries seemed to be a worthwhile exercise in accountability.

This is when 'Why are we always on last?' first emerged as a recurrent theme. Prior to the Premier League contract of 2004, we or ITV's *The Premiership* could only show extended coverage of the two (or three, if Sky had a live game) matches with more than one camera, and therefore a commentator, present. They were pre-picked and tended to feature teams at the top, or sometimes bottom, of the table. 'We're always in the round-up' cried fans of mid-table top-flight teams, as Boro often were (those were the days), and with only single-camera coverage available you might get a minute's action with a reporter summarising for the average non-feature match. When *MOTD* returned in 2004, there was a minimum camera specification at every game, so Sky and overseas broadcasters could show delayed games in full. We suggested we could do that, or show greatly extended highlights, on the new red button, but the crafty Premier League decided that could become an extra package of rights and sold it to the highest bidder, which was Sky. Even though it added to the editing bill, and we had to find some extra voices (an almost adolescent Guy Mowbray, then some way down the pecking order at ITV, was one of them), we started to send a commentator to every match and run at least a few minutes of every game. It made my job as editor much more interesting: a proper edit of any game – Portsmouth 7 Reading 4 being an extreme example – could now lead the show, and a disappointing clash between 'big clubs' could duly be demoted.

This was much fairer to viewers around the country who didn't support the big five clubs (who had traditionally dominated multi-camera coverage) and guaranteed that the running order started as a blank sheet of paper. We sat back and waited for everyone to tell us how marvellous this was. The majority of sensible viewers, who

---

13 March 2007 – FA Cup and England international rights acquired by ITV and Setanta. Deal announced by the FA's chief executive, Brian Barwick. Yes, him again.

would only get in touch with a TV programme if it wrongly accused a close relative of a serious crime, probably did approve, but in the noisy clamour of social media and message boards 'We're always in the round-up' seamlessly morphed into 'We're always on last'. Yes, Villa 0 Stoke 0 may now have been shown for six minutes with commentary, instead of 30 seconds in the old round-up, but it was last in the running order, so therefore yet another mortal slight to those clubs and their fans.

You could see it as a back-handed compliment, and indicative of how much people cared about the show and their teams, but also how football fans can instantly switch grievances. I'm reminded of an incident at a Riverside home game. Boro were playing West Ham, who won a corner in front of our North Stand. Big John Hartson, with whom I was eventually to work, was greeted with a fairly predictable 'You fat bastard'. Genial bloke that he is (unless you're Eyal Berkovic) he calmly retorted by lifting his shirt to reveal a surprisingly impressive six-pack. Without pausing for breath, the chant changed to 'You bald bastard'. John just laughed and we simply had to do the same with 'We're always on last'.

By the October of our first season back, I'd had to reply to at least one supporter (and often many more) from every single one of the 20 Premier League clubs, all convinced that we had an agenda against them. I think 15 of them claimed the running order was short-changing them – 'we're always on last'. The others were big-club fans convinced we'd been biased against them in some other way: analysing their shortcomings, praising their local rivals or only putting them on first because they'd lost unexpectedly. A journalist from the *Manchester Evening News* called Mike Whalley picked up on this thinking and started an entertaining blog called 'Last On *MOTD*' which focused on that footballing non-accolade, and usefully (for me, anyway) kept a league table which generally proved that we shared it around reasonably well. In March 2011 Birmingham radio station BRMB ran a billboard campaign with the catchy slogan 'We're Britain's second city. So why are we always on last on *Match of the Day*?' Thanks to Mike Whalley, I was instantly able to tell a panicky BBC Press Office that Birmingham City – about to be relegated with the lowest 'goals scored' tally in all four English leagues – had been on last on *MOTD* four times in seven months, while mid-table Aston Villa had been on last precisely once. In other words, an advert for a commercial rival was telling whoppers at the expense of the BBC.

Who'd have thought it? For the most part, though, I found this whole new obsession hugely entertaining, and echoed John Philips in sometimes responding to complaints with a line from a fan of another club claiming the exact opposite. And BRMB, who've since been rebranded as Free Radio, have ultimately provided the title for this book.

One even less well-founded allegation, which fortunately didn't reach the press office or the public but had got as far as the BBC director-general's office, caused me considerable alarm, then amusement, following that epic FA Cup Final of 2006. I returned to the office early the next week, relieved to have survived the *Doctor Who* scheduling trauma, only to discover that a viewer was adamant that he'd heard Mark Lawrenson say in live commentary that West Ham needed to get the ball to the 'white players'. I couldn't believe that Lawro would have said such a thing, but if he somehow had, we weren't a million miles from the scenario that had cost Ron Atkinson his job at ITV. With the director-general's office already involved, this could become a serious embarrassment and even disciplinary issue. Rightly so, if the complainant had reported it correctly. It was with a heavy heart that I sat down and watched the match recording through. Ten minutes in, after a cagey opening spell, Lawro duly pointed out to Motty that we hadn't seen much of the 'wide players' yet. On such misunderstandings can wars break out.

During that era I spent quite a bit of my week blogging, answering queries and criticisms, and mostly enjoyed the opportunity to answer back. In the end, though, I fell out with the

BBC's official line on moderating responses. I'd always embraced differences of opinion about the running order, not least because most people could spot extreme bias in other fans, and usually at least appreciated my attempts to explain. The worst that would happen is that we would respectfully have to agree to disagree. However, on 20 December 2006 (I only know because the blog's still online, it's not a date etched on my heart) I decided to try to dispel an urban myth I'd been answering on an individual basis for more than two years, and which had even found its way into the *When Saturday Comes* letters column.

This was the accusation that the commentators did not in fact travel to matches, but instead recorded their commentary on to the edit on a Saturday night to make themselves and the show look clever. This was simply not true – obviously, we could remove a misidentification later in the edit suite, but the commentator covered the game in real time, and was driving home by 6pm. Why would we send Motty to Television Centre when he could go to Selhurst Park and react to what he saw in the flesh? You could actually watch Guy Mowbray, Steve Wilson and Jonathan Pearce making on-site appearances in *Football Focus* and *Final Score* and hear them conducting interviews across our output. Or if you were there, you could look up at any Premier League gantry and see someone from the BBC with a microphone somewhere near the commentator from Sky and anyone who'd shown up from overseas. Appropriately for pantomime season, this just degenerated into 'Oh no they're not, oh yes they are', and after several days of ping-pong with the kind of people who probably think the moon landings were staged I ended the conversation with a not particularly festive, or Reithian, 'Make like a turkey and get stuffed'.

It's quite funny in retrospect (Mark Lawrenson quoted it with a chuckle for years) but I was hauled over the coals for insulting the licence payer. I couldn't see why the moderators didn't intervene when I was repeatedly accused of lying about something that was palpably true but, such was the corporate reverence for the audience, only potentially criminal or grossly offensive posts were ever removed. I thought this was nonsense and gradually stopped writing for them. Since I was churning material out voluntarily for no reward on top of the day job, I asked if I could just write online articles not blogs, but that wasn't allowed either, so I took my ball home. I was gratified to hear later that cricket correspondent Jonathan Agnew – an infinitely more high-profile and illustrious BBC Sport figure than me – had a similar ongoing debate with the social media puritans. In retrospect, it was an early and trivial example of how difficult it is for a conventional media outlet to deal with the whole fake news circus. Allowing an unfounded assertion the same credence as a factually correct, evidence-based line from one of your own journalists still doesn't strike me as the answer.

Fast forward to the autumn of 2011, and somehow I was now in charge of a Twitter account with hundreds of thousands of followers. I'd finally bought a smartphone and found myself keeping an eye on Twitter on matchdays. It was quite a useful safety net to check that we hadn't missed a story that was trending amongst fans, journalists or clubs, occasionally gave us a player quote or two in addition to the recorded interviews and provided feedback about the show in the two or three hours between coming off air and winding down and going to bed. 'I can join in this merry #bantz and post the running order in advance,' I thought, setting up the @motdeditor account. Within weeks, I had something like 300,000 followers, the club message boards were sending people with any grievance whatsoever my way, and I was unable to resist getting into squabbles with the more abusive and pig-headed ones. For some reason, how long each club featured in the opening titles that season (not much more than one second in some cases, pushing two in others) was the hot topic creating fury, and by late September I'd decided that life was too short. I can't find anything other than benign references via Google now, but it must have got a little out of hand because, once again, I was ticked off by the uber-bosses. I may have suggested that a furious Stoke tweeter was a one-eyed numpty for not spotting Peter Crouch's left ear in the opening titles, or possibly worse.

Fortunately, two things then happened: BBC Sport appointed someone to look after social media so a proper, professional @ bbcmotd account was set up – I was allowed access to post the running order and the odd fact, but no longer had to deal with the man (or woman, but almost always a man) in the street[14]– and, miraculously, Gary Lineker suddenly decided to take the plunge and set up his own account. This was a win-win all round: firstly, he soon had millions of followers, secondly, people were generally more deferential to him than they were to an anonymous editor's account, and thirdly, even when they were rude, he put them away adroitly and wittily. He still does it to this day, particularly when Piers Morgan bowls a long hop that's just begging to be despatched.

Gary's #bantzledge status became quite an asset to the programme in other ways. When Manchester City clinched the Premier League in the most dramatic fashion possible in 2012 – and Guy Mowbray and Martin Tyler held their own simultaneous 'Aguerrrrooooo' competition – I immediately asked over talkback whether Vincent Kompany would do a two-way interview from the pitch with Gary in our studio. He was their captain, a great player and a bright bloke, but, crucially, he'd been conversing regularly and amusingly with Gary on Twitter, so even though they had not yet met there was clearly a rapport there. And, indeed, it was a terrific interview at the heart of possibly the best *MOTD* I ever worked on.

On many fronts, the BBC was a better place to be towards the end of my career than when I joined. We didn't have a monopoly of sports rights any more, but we were a much better reflection of the society who paid for our services. Our on-air talent and production teams had become far more diverse, for a start. Just look at some of the 21st-century on-screen names I've mentioned in this chapter

---

14 My wife has vetoed any reference to Sid Vicious's alleged historical retort to a journalist's question about the 'man in the street'.

and the previous one and try to suggest any of them aren't there on merit. The backroom team were also no longer mostly male and 'hideously white', to use one of Greg Dyke's more contentious expressions. With an ever-greater array of competitors taking part in the domestic and international competitions we covered, BBC Sport, as the national broadcaster, had to strive to be a mirror image of both sport and the British populace. Though Channel 4 have rightly been acclaimed for their recent output, the BBC pioneered the coverage of disability sport with its extensive daily shows at Sydney 2000 and beyond. Andy Gilbert, the accomplished studio director we'll encounter later when he's caught up in an Armstrong–Hansen communication failure, was himself a former Paralympic swimming silver medallist. Then there was a subject which has become exceedingly awkward for the BBC, and many other employers, in the last couple of years – gender.

With a handful of exceptions – Viv Kent and Sharon Lence directed programmes and Wendy Shepherd and Barbara Slater directed outside broadcasts – the BBC Sport I joined had an almost entirely male senior programme-making team. Helen Rollason was about to become the first regular woman presenter, but there was scarcely a female reporter or commentator anywhere in the industry. There were women in the department – every single secretary and PA was a woman, but that was about it. It seems ridiculous looking back now, but bear in mind it was only a decade since Angela Rippon and Anna Ford had outraged a section of the British public by reading the news without a y chromosome between them. Even so, BBC Sport was clearly behind the times.

By the time I left in 2016, a woman was in charge of BBC Sport – the ex-Olympic gymnast and outside broadcast director of many sports Barbara Slater. Women were programme editing, directing matches and studio galleries and supervising match edits and analysis without anyone ever giving it a second thought. Nobody batted an eyelid any more when Gabby Logan or Jacqui Oatley presented football shows, or Clare Balding or Sue Barker fronted an Olympics or Wimbledon. And we were finally covering women's sport well beyond the Olympics and Wimbledon. To the quiet satisfaction of pioneers like the BBC's own Patricia Gregory, joint founder of the Women's Football Association back in 1969 when the FA itself still officially banned the female game, football had become the number-one participation sport amongst British girls. The England women's team didn't play its first international until the ban was lifted in 1972, a century after the first men's international. By the end of the 20th century there was a genuine desire at the BBC to cover women's tournaments properly, with ever-expanding coverage of the England team starting with highlights of their first-ever World Cup finals appearance in Sweden in 1995, and live coverage of all tournaments from Euro 2005 onwards.

The progress of the GB women's football team at London 2012 caught the public's imagination far more than the men's team did, and in due course all England's home qualifiers and a weekly *Women's Football Show* featuring extended coverage of the newly formed Women's Super League established themselves in the BBC schedules. In the last year or two, the BBC and Sky have started to integrate seasoned England internationals like Kelly Smith and her namesake Sue into their punditry on the men's game. And why not? As I occasionally point out (to little avail) when a half-wit pipes up to object on social media, no one would say that Denise Lewis or Martina Navratilova have no place on the panel when the men are competing in their sports, so why should football be different? When Alex Scott joined the BBC's FA Cup Final coverage in 2017 and subsequently appeared alongside Dan Walker and Dion Dublin at the live Fleetwood v Leicester tie, the caption '140 England caps, seven FA Cup wins with Arsenal' said it all. Plus, she's an excellent natural broadcaster.

The moment I knew things had changed for good came one Saturday in Salford when Chelsea's Eni Aluko scored in an England qualifying win live on the BBC on the same afternoon as her brother Sone scored for Hull City in the Premier League. Following the Hull edit on that evening's *Match of the Day*, Gary linked the two goals together by saying, 'In fact, it's been a good day all round for the Aluko family.' Hardly the most difficult connection to make or the most radical statement in television history; the real breakthrough as far as I was concerned came when I undertook my usual post-show masochistic trawl through Twitter. As ever, there were dozens of posts under #motd, but they were all the usual 'how could they put our rivals further up the running order than us?', 'bias [sic] analysis from Shearer again' stuff. No one had anything smart or snide whatsoever to say about showing the two siblings' goals back to back.

Progress at last, though it's still not universal. When Vicki Sparks commentated on Stoke v Everton for *MOTD* in 2018 – over a decade after Jacqui Oatley became the show's first female commentator – former ITV Sport anchor Elton Welsby tweeted that a 'lady commentator (showed) how much *MOTD* rated the Everton game'. He elaborated further during the World Cup: apparently, the 'ladies do not possess' a 'commanding and authoritative voice', the same claim made about Angela Rippon reading news bulletins in the 1970s. Poor old Elton. He should avoid TV and radio cricket commentary in particular.

A significant symbolic moment in the BBC reaching out to its audience – and one which I have to admit didn't thrill me at all when it was announced – came in 2011 when our department, plus Radio 5 Live, BBC Children's programmes and *BBC Breakfast* moved in their entirety to the brand-new BBC North complex in Salford. I did understand the principle – if you were designing the national public service broadcaster from scratch, you probably wouldn't base nearly all of it in one corner of the country, hundreds of miles from millions of licence payers. My native North East has always grumbled that 'that there London' is given undue prominence, more infrastructure investment and so on, and audience surveys historically reflected that feeling of disconnect from the BBC. Then again, everyone in Teesside always felt they were overlooked within the North East – the unimpeachably fair Roger Tames, face of ITV's regional Tyne-Tees sport, was routinely dubbed Roger Tyne down our way, despite coming from the Home Counties and supporting Arsenal.

So it was to an extent with BBC North – a BBC bigwig once tried to tell me that he'd been up to BBC Tees and that the whole region was thrilled we were moving to Salford. This was clearly tosh – it's as difficult to get to Greater Manchester from the North East as it is to get to London – and when you added in areas like Leeds and Liverpool, with their traditional hostility to all things Mancunian, the idea that the whole of the north would be won over at a stroke by some BBC departments bringing a little prestige and employment to its biggest city seemed a bit patronising. So too did the attitude of some in the BBC hierarchy. Sport was a relatively easy department to move, in that much of the coverage took place at the events, but there also seemed to be a hint of 'They all like sport up there, don't they?' about it. The (often eerily accurate) BBC spoof *W1A* summed it up in the episode when Hugh Bonneville's Ian Fletcher had to make a rare foray up to BBC North and is consoled by Jason Watkins's Simon Harwood: 'Oh I say, bad luck.' To paraphrase another great BBC comedy, *Blackadder,* there was also more than a touch of General Melchett's 'We're right behind you: 200 miles behind you' from senior management, as roughly 50 per cent of our department decided to take redundancy rather than uproot their lives.

Before anyone starts, this really was not a kneejerk 'metropolitan elite' reaction. I'm from the broader north, as were many of my colleagues (very few of us had grown up in London), and I'd had a great time in Manchester working on *A Question of Sport* back in my 20s when I had no commitments. By now, many of us had the usual responsibilities of middle age: mortgages, kids going through GCSEs, elderly parents to look after, so being uprooted anywhere wasn't going to be easy. Many senior people chose not to go – I was relatively lucky in that my wife's boss in London allowed her to work mostly from home, but others simply couldn't make it work. We lost almost our entire technical team, who were rarely with us full time but worked on other programmes and at other London-based broadcasters. Ultimately, we assembled some excellent VT editors and replacement production people from around the north, so although there were a few teething problems there were still just enough old heads to see us through. The output didn't suffer noticeably and, in any case, we were all soon back in the capital for London 2012, staying in Travelodges and the like along with many of our recently departed colleagues, and at other events like Wimbledon in due course.

There's certainly an argument that BBC Media City in Salford is already fulfilling its remit as a beacon for young talent from the north and as a counterpoint to the 'metropolitan elite' jibes which have become part of everyday political discourse, often bandied about by people who couldn't be more elite if they tried. Those who chose to leave BBC Sport all seem to have found gainful employment elsewhere and are doing fine, and those who stayed are either enjoying the social side of Manchester (the young ones) or have bought family houses they could never have afforded in London and settled in happily. But it wasn't easy at the time – some of the internal BBC North memos bordered on the Pravdaesque. They tended to start with exclamations like 'Hey gang', 'Phew!' or 'Wow!' (I wish I was joking) and invited us to 'watering holes' (meetings) while everything from the 2012 Olympic opening ceremony ('courtesy of Bury's Danny Boyle') to Hull's elevation to City of Culture status were vicariously claimed as something pan-northern for us all to celebrate. It was all very easy to parody – and some of us did, relentlessly – but there was a slightly creepy *Truman Show* feeling to it all, as if failing to be ecstatically happy in our new home wouldn't be tolerated.

The post-Hutton Report paranoia and self-examination continued before and after the move north. 'What would the *Daily Mail* think?' was formally posited in one 'watering hole' I attended as a question we should always ask ourselves before doing more or less anything. For years, the older types in our department had worried themselves silly about Charlie Sale and his 'Sports Agenda' column in the *Daily Mail*. A tiny part of me admired Charlie for hanging around at every major event and badgering his contacts in the sports industry to help him fill his daily column, the rest of me could see from a mile away who his mole was at every sports broadcaster or governing body – 'agenda' indeed – and continued to be incredulous that anyone cared what he wrote. The column was tucked away several pages from the back of the paper, and I suspect no one outside our industry has ever read it. It's far from a scientific sample, but the only time he ever wrote anything about me by name (as far as I know) he was wrong. He told his readers that I was defecting to ITV Digital not long after the BBC lost the Premier League rights in 2000. I had talked to them but decided to stay put.[15]

No BBC-related story would appear in much of the press without a barbed comment from the Tax Payers' Alliance. I've been a taxpayer for decades, but they've never consulted me before sounding off. In fact, it was (and is) a cleverly named, free-market libertarian pressure group mostly funded by anonymous donors.

An article in *The Independent* in 2016 pointed out that it shared a postal address with seven other organisations devoted to anti-EU and climate change-denying lobbying. Nevertheless, in 2009 its views – purporting to represent everyone in the UK who pays tax – were quoted in 517 *Daily Mail* articles and 307 times in *The Sun*. The Tax Payers' Alliance – and presumably, some of its anonymous backers – really don't like the BBC at all.

The post-Hutton corporation was very much on the back foot as it, and the nation, entered an era of austerity. When we were on the road covering a major event, only hotels costing less than

15 A decision at least partly influenced by my Dad reading an article suggesting that a whole digital platform based on live Football League rights might be on a less than sound financial footing. Thanks, Dad.

£100 a night (try finding one of those in Oslo) were permitted. The last time I travelled club class with the BBC was to Japan in 2002, when we went straight from Television Centre to the airport and straight to work at the other end. No one would argue that an upgrade was necessary on short-haul flights – although it would occasionally have spared some of our better-known names from being hassled – but it was now ruled out across the board, even on intercontinental trips. If you wanted to avoid travelling in economy to the Rio Olympics or World Cup, you had to pay for your own upgrade. I don't recall anyone on the production team ever feeling able to afford to do so.

I didn't go to the 2008 Beijing Olympics – it was held during the football season and I'd just spent five weeks in Vienna for Euro 2008 – but peak absurdity was achieved when a production manager struck a deal to fly everyone to China in club class for less than a rival airline was charging for economy fares. This was swiftly rejected by senior management: 'What would the *Daily Mail* think?' was, seemingly, the beginning and end of the debate. Our 6ft 4in presenter Jake Humphrey ended up briefly hospitalised with a suspected DVT having flown halfway round the world with his knees up his nose. At least we knew the *Mail* wouldn't write about that.

In my later years at BBC Sport a shift took place from simply producing television programmes for BBC One and Two. Radio Sport, or 'the wireless' as certain old-school television figures had sometimes disparagingly called it, had always been geographically and spiritually separate from TV Sport, and the twain rarely met. Occasionally a very talented person – a Des Lynam or a Clare Balding, and the odd producer – was allowed to cross the great divide, but the two media were seen as requiring totally different skill sets, so you simply weren't allowed to do both at once. These days, especially with the whole of BBC Sport housed in the same building in Salford, everyone pops up all over the place: people work on 5 Live and *Final Score* at the same time as well as blogging, running a Twitter account and passing on extra content to the website and red button. All without pausing for breath.

I would say this, wouldn't I, but today's audience gets better value for its licence fee and more respect from the modern, representative BBC Sport than it ever did back in the 'good old days'. The BBC may not have the rights to as many events, on TV at least (though that doesn't apply to radio or online) but it makes far more of what it does have. That ridiculous 1979 Saturday I cited, where England's appearance in the Cricket World Cup Final (it's only happened three times in the history of the sport) competed for airtime with four other sports on one analogue channel and scarcely made it on to *Grandstand* as a result, is unthinkable now. BBC local radio cricket online coverage means that every supporter of even a county cricket team can now hear commentary on every ball bowled all summer. When several sports take place simultaneously at an Olympic or Commonwealth Games – or several Wimbledon courts are in action at the same time – the digital and extensive online options mean that the viewer, not the editor, can choose what to watch. Admittedly the *Match of the Day* contract isn't quite like that – although the BBC's multimedia FA Cup coverage comes close – but every Premier League fan gets to see at least a few minutes' action, some quotes and studio analysis of their team, both when the show is transmitted live then all week on demand. Even if some clown of an editor always puts them on last. Time to explain in greater detail how that process works.

7.

Any Given Saturday

'So how does the programme come together?' was probably in bronze-medal position in the most frequently asked questions about my job. Gold and silver were a close-run thing between 'What's Gary Lineker really like?' and 'Why are Everton/Stoke/ Fulham/Swansea/Newcastle/West Ham/West Brom/Sunderland/ Villa/Boro/Palace/Burnley/Saints ... always on last?' The respective answers to those last two – 'He's alright, actually' and 'They're not/ won't be next season when they're in the Championship' – were generally not what the person who'd just accosted me in the kitchen at a party or in the queue for the gents wanted to hear, so I'll try to do better with that third-placed question.

During the week, *Match of the Day* has no one working exclusively on it. The Premier League contract stipulates that, in addition to the live games Sky and BT show, the BBC covers three games itself over a weekend using BBC directors and BBC-hired crews. The footage goes live to the world and is shared domestically for highlights, goal clips on your mobile and the rest of it. This needs a certain amount of planning, as does sending commentators to all the matches and organising people to fill the various matchday roles back at base, but the staff are shared across all the programmes. *Football Focus*, with an hour's worth of features and other material to find each week, is much the more labour-intensive show. The editor is the only person thinking about the content of *MOTD* during the week, and even they will have other commitments to juggle, especially as live cup ties or a big tournament loom – or the Six Nations rugby, in the case of my successor Richard Hughes.

In the post-2004 era of full coverage of all matches, the most you can do is to prepare a best-guess running order based on a pecking order of likely stories. A computer system called TIPS allows you to outline all the elements – links, VT, chat, graphics – you'll need in the show, with guesswork timings to fit the programme's overall duration. You can then amend it accordingly and relatively quickly once the games have been played. I always wrote a guide script on a Friday, in the full knowledge that Gary or I might change the wording on the day, if he'd thought of a better turn of phrase (he often had) or once we knew which games had already been shown before we linked to a particular match. They call that 'continuity' in the world of film and TV drama. We had a small amount of edit time and a producer available on a Friday for any short sequence that might set up a given match, but these were much more prevalent on *MOTD2*, where there might only be two matches on the average Sunday, so more space to build them up. My average weekday was often like a working day in any other office: organisation, admin, delegation and occasionally dealing with staff problems or managing upwards. Unlike most other jobs, though, Friday night saw us revving up rather than winding down as we built to the weekend when the showcase work was mostly done.

Saturdays were usually the biggest day of the week throughout my 27 years in BBC Sport. There was *Grandstand* for the first two-thirds of that time, then *Match of the Day* every week when we had the Premier League contract (21 of those 27 years) or just on FA Cup weekends when we didn't. Even after *Grandstand* bit the dust, there was live sport on the BBC more Saturdays than not, and from August to May we had the weekly triumvirate of *Football Focus*,

Final Score and *Match of the Day*. All three share a studio, which means sharing technical facilities and production areas, with just a little redressing of the set between shows to distinguish them from one another. The technical operation, whether in Television Centre, Salford or on the road, was always impressive, and largely a complete mystery to me.

I learnt very early on in my BBC career that camera operators and VT editors could turn a half-formed idea into something far better if you asked for their input and showed respect for their skill set. Likewise, the engineering managers, lighting and sound supervisors and others I worked with when I moved into studios kept us floundering production types afloat. The modern era of media studies graduates has seen the emergence of all-rounders who, to some extent, can combine production and technical abilities. I was under no such illusions – if anything went wrong other than editorially, I was always firmly in the hands of the techies and would try to remember to thank them when they bailed us out.

In the limited domain I liked to kid myself I did know something about, programme content, the net result of three shows sharing one studio every Saturday was editors, producers, presenters and pundits coming and going all day, sharing ideas, football gossip and in-jokes. With almost every Premier League Saturday these days featuring a lunchtime and a teatime Sky or BT live game along with all the 3pm kick-offs, this meant an absolute orgy of football from noon until 7.30pm. This was always the best part of the week as far as I was concerned. Sitting on a sofa for seven hours or so, drinking too much coffee and eating too many sweets and crisps, watching match after match with the best-informed bunch of mates imaginable.

Once we were established in Salford, we began to use a much greater variety of guests: Alan Hansen had been peerless for two decades or more, but the big contract he'd signed under Greg Dyke to secure him from would-be poachers had led to considerable pressure to use him on every show. This ubiquity eased after the move north: Hansen's eventual successor as unofficial lead pundit, Alan Shearer, was getting more confident the longer he was out of the game – especially once he'd decided not to return to management – and felt free to show more of the funny, opinionated side of his personality we'd all seen off camera for years. The audience research conducted for us after Hansen left suggested that the other Alan was now the nation's favourite pundit, so the public seem to have cottoned on to how knowledgeable and likeable a bloke he is. The latter was evident whenever his family, football friends like Shay Given or pals from outside the game came to the studios or an event. A more normal, grounded group of people it would be difficult to meet.

Alan Shearer and I cheerfully traded Tyne-Tees insults more or less as soon as he appeared on the scene – horse-punching and purple leg blotches down the Bigg Market versus heavy industry and smog monsters. Most Teessiders have cheerfully adopted the latter image – a group of Boro fans in full chemical boiler suits were often seen bewildering the locals at our away matches in Europe – and one afternoon when a wide-angle camera revealed a less than full Riverside[16], Shearer suggested a head count would improve the attendance, what with the chemically polluted air granting some Teessiders two of them. As #bantz goes, this was quite imaginative, and the least I deserved for setting the ball rolling on Gary's annual FA Cup Final variation on 'Our panel has collectively won no fewer than five FA Cups. Lee Dixon has three winners' medals and Alan Hansen has two. Alan Shearer played for Newcastle.' He's a terrific pundit, though, someone I'll always defend to the hilt and am glad to have worked alongside. So there.

---

16 Since then, Boro have done something I'd been suggesting for years and switched the camera gantry across the ground to face the always well-populated main West Stand. It makes a massive psychological difference to wider perceptions of the club. Or at least it would save me from having to point out on a regular basis that a 26,000 crowd in a town of 138,000 people was a pretty good turnout.

Sadly for us, Lee Dixon, who I'd always loved working with, especially when editing *MOTD2* with its scope for more in-depth analysis, only lasted one season with us at Salford before re-joining his former on-screen partner Adrian Chiles at ITV. We'd tried and failed to involve Danny Murphy, always a great interviewee, on a regular basis while he was still playing, but he fitted in on *MOTD* and *MOTD2* once he retired like he'd always been there as, a little later, did the excellent Jermaine Jenas. Martin Keown was quite an intense character, as he always had been on the pitch – but once he'd relaxed into the role he became a good defensively minded addition to the team. Philip Neville and Kevin Kilbane were always a pleasure to work with, and other old favourites like Ruud Gullit and Ian Wright were making welcome comebacks by the time I left the building.

To answer another FAQ, yes, the pundits do choose their own analysis, certainly the more complex themes on which they work through the evening with the assigned analysis producers. A producer or commentator will occasionally tell the editor about an outstanding performance from a player in one of the less-noticed matches, or you may be alerted to a contentious refereeing decision by a post-match managerial rant, so you might ask the pundits to assess it during the course of the evening. You then have to make sure the analysis durations will fit into your running order by making trims or prioritising amongst the pundits' chosen sequences. In purely footballing terms, you would naturally defer to their expert opinion, but as a fairly well-informed layman, I felt that if I understood the point they were making so would most of the audience, so I watched it all through in their company before the studio rehearsal with that in mind. Better still, we might learn something we wouldn't have spotted for ourselves as I often felt we would from Murphy, Shearer and Hansen at their best, and from Neville and Carragher at Sky, who use their extended airtime to great effect.

Those TV football fans who weren't around before 1992 can never appreciate how far Alan Hansen – and his fellow Scot,

Andy Gray, at Sky – moved analysis forward in the early years of the Premier League. He had been a great player in some great Liverpool teams, and his voice and manner defined 'authoritative'. Even when he said on a couple of occasions on air that the editor knew nothing about football because he supported Middlesbrough, he did it with authority. Right up to his final tournament in 2014 and that insane Brazil 1 Germany 7 game, the Hansen opinion was sought, discussed and disputed by those inside and outside the game.

It's fair to say, though, that he never entirely relished the post-2004 six- or eight-game Saturday night highlights format. Unlike, say, Alan Shearer, Mark Lawrenson or Danny Murphy, he'd never been involved outside the top half-dozen places in the league as a player and didn't really want to do so as a pundit. This was fine back when there were only two or three featured games and a round-up, but sometimes tested him slightly once any game could lead or conclude the show.

At his leaving do straight after the 2014 World Cup Final, we showed a video in which, as a semi-competent musician, I played 'Piano Man' by his favourite artist, Billy Joel, in a Rio cocktail bar (pity the poor sods who'd gone out for a romantic evening and had to suffer me plonking my way through 20 takes of that, and another dozen of the wheezy harmonica part) with rewritten lyrics contributed and sung, a line at a time, by everyone working with us out there. I changed the lines based around 'lighting up your smoke' to 'he's quick with a joke, when he's asked to watch Stoke, but there's some place that he'd rather be'. That was my small revenge for over a decade of trying to steer him away from concentrating too much on the big teams and, to be fair, he – and the lovely Hansen family who'd flown over for his TV swansong – laughed along, to our relief. Best of all, though, was Rio Ferdinand launching into a eulogy about a truly great central defender, inspired reader of the game and so on, before with perfect comic timing, pausing and adding, 'Anyway, that's enough about me ...'

That said, Alan Hansen came into his own when a really big game took place, either in highlights or live form. Where most of us would just see a great goal, he'd know immediately who hadn't tracked back or would cite an example of a similar set piece from 20 minutes ago, or last week. Back in the mid-90s, I made a montage for a late December *Match of the Day*, in the style of one of those old-school TV adverts for a dodgy K-Tel compilation album. Entitled 'Hansen's Xmas Crackers', it was basically a montage of festive graphics and the greatest goals imaginable – Carlos Alberto, Bobby Charlton v Spurs – accompanied by Alistair McGowan exclaiming things like 'terrrrible defending' and 'inexcusable' in his best Hansen/Groundskeeper Willie brogue. It culminated with Justin Fashanu's 1980 Goal of the Season for Norwich against Liverpool with a defender circled and castigated for being 'in Nae Man's Land' before Alistair/Willie/Alan muttered 'Och, it's me' and fell silent. Well, Alistair and I thought it was funny, and so did the late Tony Gubba, who presented that show.

The fact that we could send him up like that, that newspapers and managers reacted to his criticism, and that 'You'll win nothing with kids' became one of the most-quoted football lines of any era, shows how much impact Hansen made. He tried to do much more than just analyse what Basil Fawlty once called 'specialist subject: the bleeding obvious', and in the process raised the bar for all other pundits. The new generation of analysts write down something called time code displayed on a big digital clock, so producers instantly know where to find incidents from a game. Hansen lived in a different decade and just muttered, 'log that', or if all else failed, spooled up and down tapes afterwards looking for his examples. As an assistant producer, I'd often prepared his analysis sequences before becoming programme editor, and quite enjoyed the challenge of trying to second-guess his themes and look for extra clips.

On a highlights evening, Alan H would go off to VT to fine-tune his sequences, have a nap in his dressing room and then come back at rehearsal time. For a big game, he would ask for an 'overview' and then give us some cue words, at which point the studio directors with whom he'd worked most often – Phil Bigwood and later Ian Finch – would know when to run his first sequence of analysis. So when he said, 'You could have driven a bus between Arsenal's centre-backs,' incriminating evidence of Igors Stepanovs' and Gilles Grimandi's incompetence would appear, covered in lines and circles. As I became more experienced as an editor, I tended to allow more time than we'd probably need for the analysis out of the main game or two, and if we were a bit tight for time further into the show, I would gesture silently to the director next to me just to run the VT without waiting for cue words. I'd also make sure we prepared some shorter 'droppable' analysis for the later games which could either be reduced or jettisoned altogether.

On one never-to-be-forgotten (by Hansen, anyway) evening, Andy Gilbert was the rally driver to my navigator. Fortunately, I've never watched it back, and don't know the date or even year. I bet Alan does, though. He'd prepared a fiendishly subtle analysis run. Let's say he was showing how Claude Makelele provided defensive midfield cover for Chelsea – we seemed to analyse this every week for about three years, so there's a reasonable chance this was the theme. Andy and I were both expecting some pre-arranged cue words, something like 'it takes unbelievable discipline to play this role'. Hansen swears blind he'd told us something else altogether, let's say 'just in front of Terry and Carvalho'. There followed a surreal game of cat and mouse on air, with Alan repeating 'Terry and Carvalho', then pausing just long enough for Gary to think he should be asking another question. 'So, what was the key to Chelsea's victory?' he ventured, to which Hansen rambled for a couple of sentences, then returned, Tourettes-like to 'Terry and Carvalho'. After about a minute of this pantomime, with Andy and me shrugging at each other like demented Marcel Marceaux, I finally twigged that since Makelele played in front of Terry and Carvalho, this may be where he wanted to take us, so gestured to

Andy to run the VT. By this point, Alan had completely forgotten what lines and squiggles he'd added to the footage of Makelele brilliantly staying in one place all match, and a stream of twaddle was eventually spluttered out in time for Gary to link into the next game.

To his incredulity, I then said, 'Did you forget your cue words, Alan?' A decade or so later, Hansen's incredulity hasn't abated. Just as he dwelt on Liverpool's two defeats a season when he was a player instead of all the trophies, he still ignores my protestations that we successfully navigated thousands of other analysis sequences successfully. At the time, I was more bothered about the two minutes we were now over duration. To compound his unhappy evening, that meant dropping more of his carefully crafted analysis out of the later games. So there you go, West Brom and Southampton fans, our perceived failure to analyse your teams properly was as likely to be due to a collective balls-up as it was to a calculated snub.

But the really spectacular Hansen calamity, as featured in the excellent 2014 documentary *Player and Pundit*, took place at a live FA Cup tie. I do know the date of that one – Sunday, 18 February 2003 – and the game, Wolves v Rochdale in the FA Cup fifth round, our second live game of that weekend. As tends to be the case to this day when the BBC has two live games per round, the channel controllers and BBC Sport bosses pick one blockbuster which guarantees a big audience to justify the chunk of the licence fee spent on the contract, and, ideally, a second, romantic 'spirit of the FA Cup' tie. Manchester United had drawn cup-holders Arsenal, so that was scheduled for Saturday teatime, and although we generally preferred to feature a minnow playing at home, Rochdale were the smallest team left in the draw and they had never progressed beyond the fifth round, so their trip to Molineux was chosen for the Sunday teatime. It was moved to BBC Two, presumably so as not to displace *Antiques Roadshow* on One. If the geography allowed, we tended to use the same production team for both games, hiring a coach to get us to and between the venues with an overnight stay in a modestly priced hotel on the Saturday. This was a sociable way to do things – beer and wine, fish and chips or pizza on the road, and often the tail end of a wedding party in the bar when we got to the hotel. It was a chance for everyone from the secretaries who'd organised it all to the production team to Lineker, Hansen, Shearer and company to mingle and relax together. For the ex-players, this must have been something of a throwback to their playing days and they always seemed to enjoy themselves and muck in quite happily.

However, on this occasion, Alan H asked to be excused the trip between matches because he'd been invited to a 50th birthday bash in Merseyside: he'd nip across after the Old Trafford match and then make the shortish journey to Wolverhampton the next day. He was at Molineux in plenty of time, not too obviously the worse for wear, and he, Gary, Mark Lawrenson and I gathered an hour or so before the show to talk through the pre-match build-up. We'd made an opening sequence and a film about Rochdale and Lawro, always clued up on the lower leagues, was happy to talk about a historic day for them and their young player-manager Paul Simpson. To balance things up a little, we decided we'd start the studio chat with Hansen reminiscing about Molineux. He hadn't visited since his playing days, and the great old ground had been upgraded since Liverpool clinched the title there in 1979 when the back door of the dressing room opened out on to the street, allowing some resourceful away fans to join in their celebrations.

I made my way outside to join Jim Irving, our programme director, in the van. Jim was an excellent studio director, who'd learned his trade in live news, but I don't think he'd been in charge of a live football match before. The idea was that the studio team and I could show him the ropes on this routine BBC Two transmission. Rehearsal came and went – Jim worked his way through my running order. We would run titles, Gary had one line of introduction, then we'd run our opening sequence. Gary would introduce the guests and there'd be a couple of minutes' chat, beginning with the Hansen Molineux story, then Gary would link us into the Rochdale piece. We'd have a chat about the plucky minnows and by then it should be just about 'the teams are in the tunnel' time and we could hand over to the commentators. We rehearsed this a couple of times – after we'd seen the opening montage, Gary was to say 'With me at Molineux, Alan Hansen and Mark Lawrenson. Alan, you have some special memories of this fine old stadium …' Alan grunted something like, 'Yes, OK, I'll say something about the old dressing rooms in the 70s, then bring Lawro in.'

So, as we'd all done a thousand times before, we quietened down and waited for network control room and our production co-ordinator at Molineux to start their synchronised count. To minimise the kerfuffle, as programme editor, I would normally keep quiet at this point until I wanted Gary to bring the opening chat to a conclusion and get us into the Rochdale piece. We weren't particularly tight for time, as could sometimes be the case, and Gary, Alan and Mark had all been using talkback (i.e. listening to all our gallery rabbit through an earpiece) for years, so this was a well-oiled machine. In theory, that is. 'Counting to *Match of the Day* in 5-4-3-2-1, run VT,' said Jim and we were on the air. Gary led into the opening montage, our production co-ordinator, Mel Cregeen, was clear and efficient as ever, 'counting out of VT in five, four …' Somewhere in all of this, Hansen's (possibly slightly hungover) brain had short-circuited. Gary went into his scripted line, 'With me at Molineux, Alan Hansen and Mark Lawrenson. Alan, you have special memories of this fine old stadium.' Instead of springing to life with his show-stopping anecdote, he just stopped the show. Slumped in his chair, not really looking anywhere in particular, he muttered something like, 'Uh, huh, yeah. I'll say something about the dressing rooms in the 70s then bring in Lawro.'

Not knowing whether Hansen was joking, Gary tried again and elicited something even less effusive, maybe, 'Uh, huh.' By now Gary and Lawro had started to wonder if they'd misheard, and this was in fact still a rehearsal. They just looked at each other in silence, before Gary turned to camera and uttered the classic words 'Are we on the air?' There was stupefaction in the gallery: Jim, who had done everything by the book, now wondered whether he was suddenly live TV football's answer to Cloughie's line about Larry Lloyd and England caps. I took the decision to break with etiquette and join in proceedings before convention usually allowed. 'Too f-ing right we are!' I bellowed. Hansen sat bolt upright in his seat and launched into a garbled version of his anecdote which can best be described by paraphrasing Eric Morecambe's line to André Previn: 'All the right words, but not necessarily in the right order.' It was utter gibberish upon which Gary mercifully drew the curtains by linking us into the Rochdale piece.

Extraordinarily, in those pre-social media days, there was absolutely no reaction from our bosses or the press to this shambles. Along with most armchair fans, they'd watched Manchester United v Arsenal but didn't seem to have been inclined to fight for the remote control for the build-up to Wolves v Rochdale on BBC Two. The few colleagues who had seen it thought it was some strange in-joke they hadn't understood, and it never saw the light of day again until the Hansen documentary when the great man clearly felt the need to exorcise his demons and recounted 'Armstrong shouting in my ear'. Professional to the last, he's left me to relate the exact words used. And, as a lasting testament to the madness at Molineux, at the beginning of every programme he's ever presented since Gary asks the gallery pointedly as the titles are running live on the network, 'Is this for real?' Too f-ing right it is, Gary.

On the occasions when everyone realised we were on the air, a constant, but unavoidable, irritation as *Match of the Day* editor was the amount of airtime we were obliged to devote to analysing officiating decisions. Most weeks, there were at least a couple of contentious examples – sometimes more if you listened to the managers – which had a direct bearing on the results of matches. We always tried to be fair to a group of human beings who do a very difficult job to the best of their ability, especially without the benefit we had of umpteen slow-motion replays. We attempted to explain the laws of the game where appropriate (Gary has been particularly strong in this regard), and in recent times ex-refs have been made available to have an informal off-air chat with the pundits. This has helped foster a degree of mutual understanding, but the whole subject still made my heart sink on a weekly basis. I've always felt technology needed to be used in football as it is in so many other sports, but to date that's turned out to be less straightforward than I naively anticipated. VAR was a qualified success at the World Cup in Russia, but it's still goal-line technology only in the Premier League, for the 2018/19 season, at least.

It was all much less complicated back in the pre-2004 days of just two multi-camera games being linked into Television Centre at 3pm. Two pundits, usually permed from our regular three of Alan Hansen, Trevor Brooking and Mark Lawrenson, would each watch a game chosen for full coverage by the editor a couple of weeks or more in advance. It didn't matter if these two games and Sky's live lunchtime game (if there was one) all finished nil-nil, they were afforded long-edit durations and the vast majority of the analysis. Nor was the match coverage as comprehensive as it's subsequently become – cutbacks saw as few as three cameras used at some featured matches in the 1990s, whereas, for the last decade or so, the Premier League contract has stipulated a minimum of 11 at every game, plus two fixed goal-line cameras.

Pre-2004, the bulk of Saturday's games (there was no *MOTD2* until 2004, so Sunday and Monday's goals made a first BBC appearance in the following week's *Football Focus*) were recorded on single camera tapes, hand-carried to BBC regions and 'played down the line' for use in the round-up. We'd be sent these pictures by a technician, earning a spot of overtime at an empty BBC Leeds or Norwich, who quite often knew nothing about football. If a non-feature game had taken place in London, the tapes would be delivered to Television Centre and we'd have to spool up and down looking for the incidents ourselves. With only a single camera present, there was always an outside chance that the camera operator would have missed something or covered it badly. The round-up usually contained little more than goals, red cards and, if you were lucky, a great save or the woodwork being struck. Extra content like that was largely dependent either on the operator at the ground making good notes or the round-up producer at TVC keeping a close eye on the news wires for anything they thought might add to the package. With just single-camera coverage, it wasn't easy to analyse anything or for the pundits to offer up more than a sentence or two of platitudes after the round-up, usually ignoring four or five games altogether.

When you reach your 50s, you know there are many areas of life where the 'good old days' were not all they're cracked up to be. The pre-2004 *MOTD* is right up there with any of them. It was easier to edit – and I should know, I did plenty of both – but it was a far inferior editorial proposition.

Unless you were a Liverpool or Manchester United fan, or maybe Arsenal at the very end of the old show's shelf life and were served up a long edit of your team more weeks than not, the only advantage I can see looking back at the old format was the on-air voices. Gerald Sinstadt – once a fine commentator and presenter in the ITV Granada region – became a phenomenal dubber of the round-up. I went on a couple of 'writing to pictures' courses some years ago: anyone can have a stab at it, but Gerald in particular – and James Richardson on Channel 4's *Football Italia* – made it into an art form. *Match of the Day* was further blessed with two distinguished and distinctive lead commentators in John Motson and Barry Davies, and an entirely different but equally individual third voice in Tony Gubba.

Tony, having served a tough apprenticeship reporting on football in the north-west for the *Daily Mirror,* was the most fearless post-match interviewer I've ever seen. Kevin Keegan, then Newcastle's manager, once trotted out the 'I didn't see it' line after

Faustino Asprilla had elbowed Manchester City's Keith Curle in the face during a game at Maine Road. Tony retorted along the lines of, 'Well, I did see it, and it was an assault,' offered Keegan the chance to view the incriminating replays and when that was spurned, gave his own blood-curdling description. I was logging all this admiringly back at Television Centre, and half-expected Tony to re-enact the incident with Keegan playing Keith Curle and staggering off into the sunset clutching a rearranged nose himself. I'd love to have seen Tony let loose on the recent outbreak of diving in the Premier League: he'd probably have reduced the culprits to tears and made them vow on camera never to do it again.

Barry and Motty were polar opposites in terms of their styles but complemented each other beautifully. Motty was the boyishly excited enthusiast from the terraces, and the definitive football commentator in as much as you'd automatically hear his voice if you were recreating a goal in your head or throwing an obscure fact around our office.

Barry seemed to be watching from somewhere slightly loftier, he was a wordsmith with a remarkable gift for finding a line for the ages: his 'You have to say that's magnificent' in response to Maradona's second goal against England in 1986 is in its own way as perfect as Kenneth Wolstenholme's immortal 'They think it's all over ... it is now.' Not only did Barry manage to dispossess Jimmy Hill as Diego began to slalom through England's ranks but 'You have to say ...' with its overtones of 'We haven't forgotten the first goal, you little sod, but ...' spoke for the whole of England, though perhaps not the rest of the UK. And he spoke for anyone who knows anything about football with 'that's magnificent'. Barry's commentary on Dennis Bergkamp's last-gasp winner for the Netherlands in the 1998 World Cup quarter-final is as good as it gets, too. Right up there with Motty on Platini's equivalent for France in the Euro '84 semi. It helps that they're both marvellous sporting moments, but if you can turn something wonderful into something even better with just a few words, you're a pretty good commentator, and they both were.

There are some really fine BBC Football microphone-wielders in the modern era, too – Guy Mowbray, Steve Wilson and Jonathan Pearce have shared most of the big games between them since Motty retired from live TV commentary at Euro 2008, and Steve Bower, Simon Brotherton and those 5 Live regulars who sometimes appear on *MOTD* create a strength in depth that never existed in the past. The snag for all of them is that the six or seven voices heard in the course of the average modern *MOTD* are only allotted a few minutes each, whereas back in the day Motty and Barry would each have 20 minutes or more some Saturday nights. That gave them both long enough to paint some light and shade, and to establish their personalities. Jonathan Pearce is probably the best-known of the modern crop – he's instantly recognisable, as is his commentary style, and he was a key part of *Robot Wars* – but no one is ever likely to be as famous a football commentator in the future as John Motson. Nor are they likely to do it for 50 years.

Only at live FA Cup ties or the biennial summer tournament does anyone now have the chance to allow their commentary to breathe, and even then they hand to their co-commentator for an ex-pro's dissection of significant moments in the match. Barry Davies – and the great Richie Benaud in cricket – were masters of the well-chosen silence. They let the pictures talk for a few seconds after a goal or a wicket and then looked to say something apposite. Of course, that's unlikely to work in the modern, ultra-tight *MOTD* edit. The main advice I used to offer a first-time *MOTD* commentator – as well as to be themselves and not to worry if they made a mistake, because we could edit it out – was to remember that a short edit doesn't afford the natural peaks and troughs of a live broadcast. In 90 minutes there are long, uneventful interludes, so it may not jar too much if you go up a gear or two when a major incident occurs. In a six-minute edit, those peaks are all that hit the air. So, if you're a bit shouty when the ball approaches the penalty area, then make noises audible only to dogs when a genuine chance develops, the average sleepy viewer at a quarter to midnight may come to regard you as an unwelcome intruder in their living room.

In the multi-game, multi-camera universe of more recent times, visitors to the *MOTD* studio often wondered how we kept track of it all, especially from 3–5pm when there could be six or more games to watch on the stack of monitors in the production office. There were still two larger central monitors, and nominally the pundits would concentrate on a game each, but this could be swapped around as events unfolded, and we'd look to run some VT analysis of as many of the day's games as possible. Those in the production office became adept at sensing when something was about to happen on one of the screens – I, perhaps fancifully, felt the whites of the goalposts coming into view somehow attracted your peripheral vision. As the editor, I always sat on the sofa with Gary and the pundits and made notes about likely talking points and analysis themes. With the four of us, plus a studio producer and a couple of analysis producers glued to the live action, we usually had some sense of the key incidents as they occurred across the country. You could get everyone to watch the replays on the relevant monitor for an initial verdict on, say, a possible goalkeeping error or dubious refereeing decision. The studio producer would sit behind us, able to turn up the sound from any game, so we could hear a commentary reprise or fractious post-match interview and could also talk directly to any of the commentators if we wanted to compare notes with them. With *Football Focus* and *Final Score* on our monitors, too, and their production teams working in the studio next door, all three editors would keep in touch and hope to provide some continuity across the programmes. If *Final Score* had debated a subject at length, or even if *606* had taken a high volume of calls about something, it was more than likely to be a topic we'd look to touch upon in *MOTD*.

Then there was the steady flow of information needed to supplement the action. When I joined *Match of the Day,* and for a number of years afterwards, the source of all statistics on programme days – and the previous day when his detailed, typewritten match notes appeared – was the indefatigable Albert Sewell, 'our man Albert' as Des would often call him on the air. Albert had worked on Fleet Street, edited Chelsea's match programme from the late 1940s to the late 1970s and worked on *Match of the Day* longer than anyone, joining in the show's infancy in 1968 and remaining a fixture for more than four decades. As a young editor I often turned to him as a sounding board and arbiter of good grammar and sound journalism. When Albert died in June 2018, aged 90, amidst the mourning we reflected that the last Chelsea game of his lifetime fittingly saw them lift the FA Cup and that the last England game he'd watched was a national World Cup record 6-1 win against Panama. Albert retired at the time of the move to Salford, but his philosophy and gentlemanly presence was always with a generation of us, including the young journalists we recruited to unearth our stats in the computer era.

That back-up and the comprehensive information now available at an editor's fingertips helps ensure that *Match of the Day* is journalistically sound, controversial running orders notwithstanding. The presence of a commentator at every game – even if some social media refuseniks thought otherwise – BBC directors at three of them, and a dedicated producer in VT at the studio for each game also gives the editor a reassuring safety net. You could talk to any of these people at any juncture, and I made a point of speaking to all of them once the games were over. I never minded hearing from four different people that Dimitri Payet had lit up a dull game or that Phil Brown had blown a gasket post-match. Far better a little repetition than learning for the first time about something significant in the next day's papers or on Sky's *Goals on Sunday*. Having weighed up all the ingredients, my provisional running order, including approximate durations and proposed analysis, would come together by about six o'clock, but was not set in stone until full time in the teatime game.

No one factor ever determined the running order: later in the season, the title race was likely to feature at the beginning of the show, in all probability followed by the relegation candidates and the battle for European qualification. Early in the season, you'd try to have a considered look at the promoted teams and those who'd got off to a flier. Then there were often other issues at play: big-name signings making their debuts, or managerial comings and goings. The number of goals in a game also came into play, unsurprisingly: high-scoring matches tended to shoot up the running order and – much as we wanted to provide thrilling entertainment all the way until midnight – one 0-0 draw per Saturday, especially if it was between two mid-table sides, was not necessarily unwelcome. Or, better still, there'd be a 1-1 on a day otherwise overflowing with victories: either of those scenarios and the 'last on *MOTD*' conundrum was usually solved at a stroke. Gary Lineker is telling the truth when he tweets to say he's not responsible for the running order. The editor quite rightly carries the can, but on those occasions when the pecking order of matches was less than clear cut, I generally ran it past Gary, as a well-qualified sounding board who'd be the public face of the final verdict. Ultimately, though, especially if it makes you feel better, I'm the person who always put your team on last.

As I mentioned earlier, each game was, and still is, assigned its own producer. That person logs all the incidents and timecodes throughout the afternoon, liaises throughout with the commentator on site then spends the evening with a proper editor, a skilled videotape editor, mixing the sound to smooth over the joins, and trimming the game and interviews to the duration assigned by the other, non-technical, programme editor. I oversaw these match edits for years before moving to studio duties, so was always aware of how complex they are. By 10.30pm on a Saturday, there can easily be 100 or more individual edits in a ten-minute package. Every corner or free kick will be tightened to remove the delay between award and restart, replays are switched to ensure the best angle is used and commentary is shortened and moved around as appropriate, but not added on to the edit afterwards. Parkinson's Law applies in that an edit will take as long to put together as the time there is available – midweek *MOTDs* always make it on to the air but the edits are understandably less polished.

Intercutting matches only really came into play at the end of the season, and even then only when an afternoon ebbed and flowed to such an extent that the story could only be told fully by crossing chronologically from match to match. Two memorable examples spring to mind: that 'Aguerrroooo' afternoon in 2012 where Manchester City snatched the title from neighbours United by putting two goals past QPR in injury time, and an extraordinary last-day relegation battle in 2005. Bryan Robson's West Bromwich Albion had been adrift at the bottom of the table for months but an unlikely late run of results had left them with a chance of a last-day escape.

For the first time since the advent of the Premier League, no one had been relegated prior to that final day: Albion were still bottom, with Southampton, Crystal Palace and Norwich just above them, and still in mortal danger. Only one of those four could escape, but on a scarcely credible afternoon where all four were at one time or another above the drop zone, the last of many seemingly pivotal moments came when Charlton equalised with eight minutes of the season left to relegate Palace and save West Brom. I edited that show, but a complex relegation package of something like 20 or 30 twists and turns where one commentator's summary led to a mini-table graphic, anxious fans listening to the radio and the next incident from somewhere else, was masterminded by the regular *MOTD2* editor of that era, Mark Demuth. Mark's a lifelong Palace supporter, so had to remain supremely professional and suspend his heartache until his magnum opus had been transmitted. Much as I did when Boro went down on another topsy-turvy last day of the 2008/09 season. And 1992/93 and 1996/97, come to think of it. I'd left by 2016/17.

On at least one other occasion, a potential intercut was shelved on the grounds that the anticipated rollercoaster ride hadn't materialised. On the final day of the 2009/10 season, table-topping Chelsea needed to beat Wigan at home to be crowned Premier League champions, otherwise Manchester United would retain their title if they defeated Stoke. If United scored first, both games remained scoreless for a while, or even if Chelsea were just a goal ahead late in their game, there'd be tension, fans anxiously checking their phones for score updates and every reason to edit the two games together into one package. None of these scenarios materialised: Nicolas Anelka put Chelsea ahead after six minutes, and they cantered to an 8-0 victory and duly picked up the trophy. News of this romp quickly filtered through to Old Trafford, where the atmosphere went flat as United eventually registered a rather hollow 4-0 win. I abandoned any thoughts of an intercut and led the show with the new champions, eight-goal Chelsea. One of the easier editorial decisions in the programme's history, or so I thought. Over the next few days, I found myself having to reply, as politely as I could, to emails from viewers who'd wanted us to intercut or create an entirely false dramatic narrative by running the United game first. Even if you were one of that diminishing breed who emulates that *Likely Lads* episode and avoids the results all day, the polite handshakes after each goal at Old Trafford would have given the game away. One emailer in particular, though, exploded with anger at the decision and entered into a correspondence with me, through our complaints unit, which went on for several weeks. One of my weary closing lines – 'your bandying of words such as "stupid" and "clown" is perhaps misplaced' – rather sums up that futile exchange.

Compared to the lunacy of *Sportsnight*, a modern midweek *Match of the Day*, while often livelier and less finessed than its Saturday equivalent, benefits both from modern technology and the extra preparation time granted by following what is now the *Ten O'clock News*. The only unusually stressful night I can remember on one of those shows came in December 2010, during our last season at Television Centre. There was a power cut in the rickety – and by now rodent-infested – old building at about 8.45pm, which took out our VT operation for almost the whole second half of all the games. If it had continued for much longer we might conceivably have had to cancel the show, but with power restored about an hour before transmission, we were thrown back into a *Sportsnight* mode of cobbling together whatever we could, in whatever order we could. The three BBC outside broadcasts had been alerted immediately we knew there was a problem, so had recorded full coverage on site and played clips down the line for a rapid turnaround once power was restored.

Unfortunately, the biggest story of the night – bottom-of-the-table Wolves winning at Anfield for the first time in decades with a second-half Richard Stearman goal – was a Sky game. As was always the case in my experience of our operational partnership, the Sky people on site were extremely helpful, recording the game and our commentary for us locally as soon as we alerted them to our problems. Clearly, they couldn't interrupt their own broadcast to play this to us, so we had to wait until they were off the air to be sent any of it. We managed to rustle up an edit which, mercifully, included the goal and a quote from the victorious manager Mick McCarthy, but it was a brief and threadbare package far removed from our usual standards. Unlike our previous *MOTD* Molineux mess – the Hansen brain fade which somehow went unnoticed – there was considerable overnight disquiet in the Black Country. Fortunately, once it was explained, Wolves themselves were great about it – I threw myself on the mercy of the court, wrote something for their club website and had a chat with the *Express & Star* and local radio. I belatedly discovered that even partisan football fans can be surprisingly reasonable when you hold your hands up and apologise. Sometimes, at least.

The other sea change in 2004 was the granting to the BBC of a Sunday night highlights programme. From the Premier League's inception, Sky had moved one of each weekend's best matches, including many of the big encounters of the season, to Sunday at 4pm. There was now to be another live TV game earlier on a Sunday and with the UEFA Cup, later rebranded as the Europa League, moving to Thursday nights, some weekends saw several fixtures move back a day. This show was initially a BBC Two proposition; *Top of the Pops* had a spin-off show called *TOTP2* on that channel, so *MOTD2* became our new show's title. Fifteen years later (a terrifying thought, where did that decade and a half go?), the name seems to have stuck. Quite a lot of effort went into making it different from its Saturday night older brother. There was a contractual stipulation that any edit of a Sky live game couldn't contain any more than ten minutes of match action. This opened the door for VT set-ups for each game, extended analysis afterwards, a full round-up of the previous day's action and a weekly feature which usually included comedian Kevin Day finding a quirky story at one of Saturday's games.

The show was staffed from within our existing production team – I generally edited one show a month – but Mark Demuth was put in charge and edited it most Sundays. The main presenter – chosen, as they tend to be, at the very top of our department with input from the channel controller – was to be Adrian Chiles, a dryly humorous long-suffering West Brom supporter who'd previously been the face of BBC business programmes. Saturday's frontman was a famous ex-pro, Sunday's was going to voice the round-up and ask questions of the pundits from a fan's perspective. Mark had previously had a spell in charge of BBC Solent Sport where he'd struck up a rapport with the then Southampton manager Gordon Strachan, who duly became the football-savvy ying to Adrian's layman yang. As a Boro fan, it's unfortunately become customary to hear Strachan derided. He had an unsuccessful year as our manager, which, if nothing else, proved how far Scottish club football had fallen. Back in the 70s and 80s, Dalglish, Hansen, Souness and Gordon himself came to England and shone. In 2009, Gordon, following a silverware-heavy spell in charge of Celtic, brought several of the leading lights from the Old Firm to Teesside with him, and watched on in horror as most of them stank out the English second tier. But as a pundit, a foil for Adrian and good company on a Sunday, Gordon was an inspired choice to help us establish the new show. He also turned down the severance pay he was entitled to from Middlesbrough, saying he felt he hadn't earned it, which is the mark of the man.

When Gordon went back into management, he warned us all that the nice guy we'd been working with would revert to the touchy boss who'd once (hilariously, to be fair) asked our delightful, but occasionally long-winded, reporter Garth Crooks to start the post-match interview as he walked down the tunnel. Gordon's rationale was that he could nip into the dressing room to see his team but still be back in time for the end of Garth's first question. Lee Dixon was the next regular *MOTD2* pundit – as I've already said, he was an absolute natural and soon became part of our panel for England games and one of the best TV football analysts in the country. Then Lee's sparring partner Adrian left, but again a distinctive replacement was found in Colin Murray. And after Colin came that fine operator Mark Chapman. The three of them – and their radically different styles – illustrate why I've always struggled to answer another question I've been asked many times over the years: what makes a good presenter? It's entirely subjective: I've worked with every high-profile presenter BBC Sport has employed in the last three decades, and I really couldn't give you a definitive answer.

Some have an easy rapport with (most of) the public, a twinkle in the eye and a touch of self-deprecation: Gary, Des (from whom Gary learnt a great deal), Gabby Logan, Clare Balding, Dan Walker and Mike Neville from my *Look North* days would all fall into that category. I wasn't around when Mike started to present in Newcastle, but I do know, from watching Des and most of the others in their early TV appearances and from working with Gary in his, that while they were all competent from the outset, none of them burst onto the screen as the finished article. Like any other craft, you have to master the basics before you can innovate and improvise. Even the Beatles released 'Love Me Do' first, then worked their way up to *Revolver* and *Sergeant Pepper*. The bottom line with any presenter is competence and an ability to get a show out of a hole, preferably without the viewers even knowing you've been in one in the first place. Some of the less flamboyant presenters I've worked with – Steve Rider, Sue Barker, Mark Pougatch – were amongst the best. All technically brilliant, easy-going and calm. It's unfair to categorise them as 'safe pairs of hands' because they were so much more than that. Then there were the mavericks – David Coleman, Esther Rantzen, Ray Stubbs, Adrian Chiles, Colin Murray – with bags of personality and drive, and 19 thoughts and ideas to the dozen. It's no bad thing to have a mixture of all of the above on a presentation team, or indeed as colleagues during the course of a career.

In my later years at BBC Sport, I quite often edited our afternoon scores and results service, *Final Score*. When that's going well and Mark Chapman or Jason Mohammad, with thousands of hours of live radio under their belts, confirm what a goal update from a reporter at the ground means for the league table before you've even managed to mutter it in their ear, the afternoon flies by.

There's an adrenaline rush of a different kind when it goes wrong, though. One of my favourite studio directors to sit beside was the ultra-organised, calm and authoritative Kelly Faulkner who, though she directed the World Cup Final studio in Russia in 2018, worked primarily on *Final Score* during my time in Salford. In late April 2014 we were jointly tasked with steering Dan Walker through a Premier League Saturday, which also happened to stage the penultimate set of Football League fixtures. I'm one of those anoraks who quite likes a set of permutations, our excellent researchers had produced the usual comprehensive briefing document explaining who could go up, down or into the play-offs, and what combination of results would cause any of that to happen.

During Italia '90, I'd been branded a 'trainspotter' by Brian Barwick for working out that when Romania equalised in the final group game against Argentina, the latter were still going through as it stood, as one of the highest four third-placed teams. Because of the way the fixtures had fallen, if it finished 1-1 they couldn't be overhauled by enough of the teams still to play in the other groups. Viv Kent eventually understood my reasoning over talkback and passed it on. I guess that phrase was Brian's version of a wry back-handed compliment, but, either way, confirming that the World Cup holders were safely through before coming off the air seemed like good public-service TV, even if it was trainspotterish.

For this 2014 *Final Score*, I'd printed out all the pre-kick-off railway timetables, sorry, league tables, ostensibly so I could confirm our 'as it stands' computer graphics to my own satisfaction and perhaps give Dan an extra stat or two in his ear. All was going well until about midway through the second half when the whole of the computer information system crashed. We were suddenly back in the era of David Coleman presenting *Grandstand* in the 60s and 70s, except David always had a basic teleprinter to read and had made learning every conceivable statistic by rote – 'Forfar unbeaten now in six games' – a badge of honour. Dan is good, but he'd never anticipated he'd have to be that good. It became clear that this was a major fault in a central database somewhere beyond the BBC: there would be no score graphics or 'as it stands' tables any time soon. You only have to watch one of those airport or railway network 'fly on the wall' documentaries to know that computers are great when they work, but when they fail, they tend to fail completely. There's usually no halfway house.

We quickly established that Jeff Stelling's *Soccer Saturday* team at Sky were experiencing the same problem, otherwise I'd have watched their output and passed what I could on to Dan – I'm not proud. Instead, we did what sports desks must have done back in the 1930s – I took the league tables I'd printed off and began to scribble my own 'as it stands' tables on bits of paper, amending points tallies and goal difference[17] as score updates came in. We had a reporter in a press box at every game in the Premier League and Championship, and they were usually quick to know the implications of their latest score for the wider division. All the same, I frantically cross-checked my bits of paper whenever we went across to any of them. More worryingly, we only had one reporter available in each of Leagues One and Two and weren't being alerted in the usual way if a goal went in anywhere else. Not ideal on a day when teams' fates were being settled.

Everyone mucked in – the graphics operators, deprived of their usual life-support systems, monitored BBC local radio and club social media accounts, then shouted through score updates over talkback. In a perverse way, it was quite enjoyable – Dan is one of the least precious people you'll ever meet and calmly told viewers that our normal in-vision score service was kaput, but that we'd do the best we could. If you handle these things with humility – Des's line 'you love it when that happens' springs to mind – the public will usually side with you. Kelly and I had the small consolation of knowing that however bad it got we could walk the streets afterwards without anyone knowing we'd been involved, unlike Dan. That's one of many reasons why presenters earn more money than production people. Also, as editor and producer we had a lot of programmes under our belts between us – you really wouldn't want that to happen during your first show in charge. Firstly, you'd probably panic, and secondly (and entirely unfairly) you'd find yourself associated with it, and possibly be put off live galleries for life. We weren't at that stage of our careers, but it was still a new situation for everyone involved.

As the final whistles started to blow, I frantically triple-checked the scribble on my league tables. I really didn't want us to be responsible for giving any set of fans misinformation about

---

17 If we had really recreated an authentic 1930s sports desk, then goal average – goals scored divided by goals conceded – would have been employed instead of goal difference, and I would have been reduced to a gibbering wreck.

their team, especially at this crucial moment in the season. The details mostly escape me now, but I do remember telling Dan that he could confirm to the BBC One audience that Rochdale had been promoted and that Carlisle were hanging by a thread as they tried to avoid going in the opposite direction. I think we had some form of full-time scores visual available for the classified results sequence and we came off the air without erroneously promoting or relegating anyone. The television equivalent of *Withnail and I's* 'We've gone on holiday by mistake' was narrowly avoided.

Nothing quite as exciting as that ever happened on the air during my more numerous Saturday *MOTD* editorial outings – most weeks it went pretty smoothly, with nothing worse than an occasional run of analysis having to be dropped when the live chat durations exceeded my estimates. Every now and then, though, something unforeseen would arise. I was editing *Match of the Day* in 2012 when Liverpool's Luis Suarez refused to shake Patrice Evra's hand, having previously been suspended for eight matches for racially abusing the Manchester United full-back. The game of football could have done without this episode, as it could have done without the three biting incidents in Suarez's career. I was not the kind of editor who relished covering dismal behaviour which would probably migrate from the back page of the papers to the front – I preferred us to transmit football action – but we all knew it was a big story and that we had to do it justice. My heart sank even further when Liverpool manager Kenny Dalglish denied that anything untoward had happened and berated Sky's Geoff Shreeves for having suggested that it had. Ultimately, Kenny – a really good man, with whom we'd worked during Italia '90 and Celtic's run to the 2003 UEFA Cup Final – realised his loyalty to Suarez had been betrayed once again and apologised for his initial reaction, but, in the meantime, he phoned his close friend Alan Hansen that evening. He then texted a still photo which was doing the rounds: this seemed to suggest that Suarez had in fact tried to shake hands.

Alan and I examined the corresponding VT pictures frame by frame and realised that this was an optical illusion, a photo taken the split second before the Uruguayan withdrew his hand. To his credit, Alan went on the air and rightly said that Suarez's behaviour had been indefensible, but it wasn't easy for him to do so, and make Kenny look foolish in the process. I loved watching that era's peerless Barcelona team of Xavi, Iniesta and Messi – and their glorious, largely cynicism-free approach – but have never warmed to the club quite as much since Chewy Luis arrived at the Camp Nou.

The Dalglish–Shreeves exchange also presented *Match of the Day* with a dilemma. Back in 1995 I'd logged a Manchester United versus Middlesbrough game for *MOTD* in which Roy Keane was shown a second red card in a few weeks for lashing out at Jan Aage Fjortoft. John Motson, entirely reasonably it seemed to me, asked Alex Ferguson (he wasn't Sir Alex yet) how he planned to address Keane's discipline problem. This provoked an angry response and the interview was abruptly terminated. There was then a debate about whether we should include any of this in the VT package – it was well above my pay grade as an assistant producer to adjudicate – and though Des Lynam floated the idea of running it with a Fergie expletive beeped out, in the end editor Brian Barwick chose not to do so, though Keane would be castigated by our pundits. I understood this decision – it was a heat of the moment flash of temper from Fergie, he would doubtless calm down and all would probably be well the next time *MOTD* came calling. When (the by now) Sir Alex eventually did stop talking to the BBC altogether in 2004, it wasn't BBC Sport's doing. A BBC Three documentary about his football agent son, Jason, to which Ferguson senior took exception, meant one of football's greatest-ever managers didn't speak to the BBC for seven years.

The Dalglish interview – though also an over-protective defence of an errant player – was different. It had been shown live on Sky, so was already in the public domain. I phoned Tony Mills, Sky's football executive, and asked if we could use it. He said yes, so we ran part of it in *MOTD*. One or two people at the BBC weren't convinced that we should have rerun a Sky 'scoop', but I just thought it was an important part of the overall story and that we'd simply been grown-up in acknowledging the newsworthiness of someone else's interview after their live game. I also take umbrage when TV news organisations, including the BBC, bang on about landing an 'exclusive'. It's either worth its place in the running order, or it isn't.

Other occasions when Saturday evenings became unexpectedly lively included Gary Lineker recording a phone interview with Bobby Robson for *MOTD* when it emerged in 2000 that the FA had asked him to replace Kevin Keegan as England manager. Bobby explained why he was staying at Newcastle, and we rapidly trimmed a match edit or two to accommodate him on *MOTD*. I guess that was an 'exclusive', but we didn't bill it as such. Sometimes, we'd find ourselves on the receiving end of an interesting call. One Saturday in 1999, when I was deputising for Niall Sloane, Chelsea's Graeme Le Saux was put through to the editor's phone by the BBC switchboard. Earlier that day he'd hit Liverpool's Robbie Fowler (off the ball and undetected by the match officials) after Fowler had repeatedly pointed his backside at him. Society has evolved somewhat in the last two decades and so, by his own admission, has Fowler. At the time, however, Le Saux, despite being happily married with two children, had occasionally found himself subjected to homophobic abuse. This largely, it seems, was his punishment for acts of footballer nonconformity like listening to indie music, visiting art galleries and reading *The Guardian*. Graeme suspected that our cameras must have caught him lashing out, so knew he'd be in trouble, but he just wanted to make sure we'd also clocked what had provoked him. I reassured him that we had and that we would be showing it in full, as indeed we did.

Then in 2008 I was contacted one Saturday evening by Arsenal's media chief, Amanda Docherty, who wanted to send us a statement from Arsene Wenger. Arsenal's striker Eduardo da

Silva had suffered a broken leg that afternoon so gruesome we'd frozen the slow-motion replay to avoid the grisly aftermath and had already decided to remove even that sanitised replay from the pre-watershed Sunday morning repeat. A distressed Arsenal coach had initially squarely blamed Birmingham defender Martin Taylor for the injury, but on reflection Arsene had concluded, as had our pundits, that though it was clearly a red card offence, it was down to poor timing rather than any intent to hurt an opponent. The damage caused was still awful but we were able to defuse a potential blame game and gave Wenger credit for retracting his original comments. As editor, I was relieved that we'd averted a fruitless feud. Much the most important consideration was Eduardo's welfare. I'd never have made a tabloid journalist. As Chris Morris's news anchor yelled at hapless reporter Peter O'Hanraha-hanrahan on *The Day Today*, 'Peter, you've lost the news' Or, as the great cricket writer and broadcaster John Arlott once put it, 'Some people take life too lightly and sport too seriously.'

So, for anyone who ever asked that question 'How does the programme come together?', there you have it. That was the Saturday job.

8.

Off Script

As a rule of thumb at BBC Sport, other than at major events where we generally worked right through the entire duration, the rota would usually allow us one weekend a month off. In other words, we worked something like 40 weekends a year. In nearly 27 years there, that's more than 1,000 Saturday shows, plus hundreds more on Sundays, Wednesdays and Bank Holidays and during tournaments. The vast majority of those centred around football, and most of those were programmes called *Match of the Day*.

It was rarely routine, but there was a pattern to the week and a formula to assembling the shows when I was part of the production team, then as custodian of our great old flagship. Even so, in over a quarter of a century working for the same employer, there were times when I found myself a long way from the match edit/studio gallery safety net. I've just Googled 'comfort zone' in the hope of finding an apposite quotation, but they're pretty much all from screen actors who seem to think they should be awarded a purple heart for playing slightly against type. American author Neale Donald Walsch says, 'Life begins at the end of your comfort zone', which is promising enough, until you then read that he also claims to know the 'Three Secrets to Everything'. Perhaps I should avoid airport bookstall spirituality and relate some examples instead.

It's April 1994 and I'm on the pitch at Bootham Crescent, home of York City, with a cameraman and that fine old-school British character actor – one I suspect never wittered on about his comfort zone – Brian Glover. On my cue, Brian is about to recreate one of British cinema's finest scenes as he resumes the role of the over-zealous games teacher from Ken Loach's *Kes*. In the goalmouth, a cardboard cut-out of Sylvester Stallone in his *Escape to Victory* goalkeeper's outfit is about to fail to save from Brian, whose exaggerated celebration – 'And that, boys, is how to take a penalty' – will take him alongside our presenter Clare Grogan (of *Gregory's Girl* fame) who's then going to link us into a set of archive football film clips. Three iconic football film references all squeezed into one sequence. And if this doesn't seem like an effective use of the licence fee, we'd already shot a sequence that day with ex-World Cup and *It's a Knockout* referee Arthur Ellis brandishing a red card at Clare in his garden elsewhere in Yorkshire. Value for money, or what?

This was *The Beautiful Frame,* my contribution to *Goal TV,* a one-off football-themed evening BBC Two allowed BBC Sport to make. I dug out the reference books and researched every film or TV drama I could find that contained any of those generally laughably bad reconstructions of match action, cameo appearances by footballers (almost all laughably bad, too, with the exception of Graeme Souness in *Boys from the Blackstuff*) or football spectator sequences: 'Going to t'match' being a staple component of early British kitchen-sink scripts. I watched maybe 100 movies and TV dramas in a month or so – not exactly a chore – and ended up with mountains of suitable footage, ranging from JB Priestley to Alf Garnett. I grouped these into themes and, with the rare freedom to structure it all as I chose, started to dream up some far-fetched links like the ones above. All the clips of the old British films cost a standard fee, something like £250 per minute, to include them in the finished piece. *Escape to Victory* was owned by Hollywood giants Paramount who wouldn't budge from their standard fee of several thousand pounds per minute. Hammy nonsense though it was, it was probably the most famous film on the list, so I decided to include it by way of the life-sized Stallone cut-out. I took immense satisfaction in volleying the ball into his midriff and knocking him into the net for the final shot in the credits before we wrapped our filming at York City.

I'd asked Clare Grogan to present: she had been a pop star of some note with Altered Images, and a female icon as far as my generation was concerned, having starred as Gregory's eventual love interest in possibly the best football film of the lot. Her Glaswegian cousin, Steve McBride, was a colleague of mine so had her phone number, which helped. My moustachioed Arsenal-supporting friend from schooldays, Chris Wise, had by now graduated from the Schoolboy's Enclosure to being proud holder of Arsenal North Bank season ticket number 001, for which he queued up early every year when they went on sale. He was now my flatmate in Shepherd's Bush, and in those pre-mobile phone times came home late one night to a message on our answerphone from Clare Grogan. Once he learned this wasn't a prank call and that Clare and I were about to do some work together, this gained me more street cred in Chris's eyes than the rest of my career put together.

My other contribution to *Goal TV* was to suggest that Ray Davies should write the theme tune. As a teenager in the late 70s, fan of The Jam and would-be guitarist, I'd followed Paul Weller's musical recommendations assiduously. When he said 'Waterloo Sunset' by the Kinks was his favourite song – a fine choice, it'll be one of my *Desert Island Discs* in the unlikely event I'm ever invited on – and that Ray Davies was a truly great songwriter, I started to trawl the back catalogue of this most English of figures. He'd written another song, 'Autumn Almanac', through the eyes of a man who'd lived in the same street all his life, liked roast beef on Sunday, holidaying in Blackpool and 'my football on a Saturday'. It was a perfect portrait of my Granddad's generation, indeed of my paternal Granddad himself. I knew Ray was a big Arsenal fan – a genuine one who'd travelled home and away to watch them in their double-winning season of 1970/71, and whom we later saw on our plane back from Copenhagen after they'd lost the 2000 UEFA Cup Final to Galatasaray – so I thought it might appeal to him.

Ray duly agreed to write the music, and Stuart Cabb – later to produce Louis Theroux's *When Louis Met* documentaries – and I went to Crouch End to see him in his Konk Studios. Technically, I didn't need to be there since Stuart was making the titles and other sequences around our individual programmes, but I invited myself along anyway, since it had been my idea and I was keen to meet someone I greatly admired. Ray was gentle, polite and serious. He picked up what he described as his 'Django Reinhart' guitar – maybe the great Django had once owned it, but either way it had that lovely twangy 30s sound – and played us what he'd written, as if it was an audition and we had any right to criticise. I was thrilled that he'd taken the football line from 'Autumn Almanac' and turned it into a lament about the demise of the North Bank (my flatmate's season ticket would have a row and seat number on it instead of just 001 from now on) with the refrain 'The terraces are gone'. As a theme tune for a full evening of all manner of football nostalgia and creativity – *The Beautiful Frame* was actually one of the less arty elements – it was perfect.

Documentary making ebbed and flowed during my time at BBC Sport – the regular conveyor belt of channel controllers meant they sometimes trusted the horny-handed sons and daughters of sporting toil to branch out, and sometimes didn't. Alan Hansen made a string of football documentaries, they'd snap up an opportunity like *When Lineker Met Maradona*, we'd be allowed to celebrate the career of one of our own like Coleman, Motson or Davies, and Jo McCusker made some superb film profiles of sporting greats from Seve Ballesteros to Sir Bobby Robson. Either way, once you'd moved upstairs to work regularly in galleries, your chance to work on these productions had gone. Fortunately for me, the mid-90s and the success of *Goal TV* presented a couple of other opportunities to trawl the archives and meet some sporting history makers.

1996 saw the centenary of the modern Olympics movement, and BBC One commissioned an all-encompassing tour de force called *The Essential Olympics* to run shortly before the Atlanta Games. A whole team of producers and researchers worked on this production. With the end of the football season and Euro '96 coming up, I wasn't going to be involved in putting the final programme together, but I was allocated the rewarding task of finding as many veteran British Olympians as possible from the 1950s and beyond. The British Olympic Association had a comprehensive list of those who were still alive and Mark Demuth, employing his interviewing skills from his earlier career at Hayter's News Agency, and I went off around the country to track down the gentlemen (they were almost all male) amateurs of a bygone era.

First, we spent the day with Sir Harry Llewellyn, the aristocratic showjumper who clinched Britain's only gold of the Helsinki Games of 1952 with a clear round on his horse, Foxhunter. We took Sir Harry up to the Brecon Beacons to film a poignant sequence at Foxhunter's graveside. Then we interviewed Sir Daniel Pettit, who had played for the GB football team at the 1936 Olympics. The England international team had been obliged by the FA to salute Hitler on a visit to Germany the previous year, but Sir Daniel and his colleagues decided to do no such thing. He'd then been present when the great Jesse Owens undermined the Führer's demented theories of racial supremacy and entered Olympic folklore.

The oldest of all the Olympians we found was a truly memorable figure. Rowland George was in his 90s and living in a nursing home in Somerset, but immediately invited us to come and see him when I phoned. In 1932 he'd been a member of the winning coxless four at the Henley Regatta. They were casually asked by the authorities afterwards if they'd fancy rowing for Great Britain in Los Angeles later that summer. This gallant quartet dropped everything and set off across the Atlantic by steamer, taking their boat with them, and crossed Canada by train. They stopped off for a spot of practice whenever there was a convenient lake nearby, arrived in LA just in time for their event and duly won gold.

Rowland happily recounted all of this and was thrilled when I handed him a VHS tape. We'd found the footage of his race from 64 years earlier in one of the newsreel archives and made him a copy. He'd never seen it before, and subsequently sent me a beautifully handwritten note thanking the 'ingenuity of the BBC' for unearthing it for him. One final, very touching, detail: when we arrived at the care home and were shown into his room to set up our camera, Rowland George greeted us wearing the official GB Olympic team blazer and tie he'd been given back in 1932. What he didn't tell us – and this is typical of that generation – was that he was much, much more than just a sporting hero. Rowland was appointed OBE in 1943 for his role as an RAF squadron leader in North Africa during Operation Torch. He was then in charge of the Allied supply system from the beaches to the airfields during the Salerno landings in Italy, successfully carrying out his duties despite being wounded under fire. He was mentioned twice in dispatches, and subsequently received the Distinguished Service Order and the US Legion of Merit.

A few years later, I represented *Match of the Day* at a memorial service for its first-ever presenter and commentator Kenneth Wolstenholme. An ex-RAF colleague described how as a bomber pilot in the low-flying Pathfinder squadron, Kenneth had flown exactly 100 missions over Germany during World War Two. The death toll was such that surviving 25 missions was regarded as highly unusual. Even the BBC old-timers present were astonished to hear this account – Kenneth had never spoken about it to any of them. No wonder his football commentaries sounded like he was enjoying himself, rather than viewing it as life and death. He must have found it odd to hear other journalists' accounts of bravery and heroism in the sporting arena. There are heroes, and then there are real heroes.

The Essential Olympics having been deemed a success, the following year, with the BBC about to lose the live rights for the first time since the FA Cup Final was originally televised in the 1930s, BBC One commissioned *The Essential FA Cup Final*. This time, I was part of the team putting it together – Graham Wellham, Tony Pastor and I divided the filming and editing between us, Mark Demuth again did most of the interviewing and we trawled the country interviewing everyone from the absurdly modest gentleman knights, Sir Stanley Matthews and Sir Bobby Charlton, to FA Cup Final goalscorers from Roger Osborne of Ipswich to Keith Houchen of Coventry. Even the more recent winners recalled their golden moments with a childlike glee; these victories were, in most cases, the pinnacle of their careers. Sadly, with the notable exception of Wigan's triumph in 2013, those romantic stories have been almost entirely absent in the last two decades or so. Arsene Wenger's recent achievement of three FA Cup wins in four years is scarcely even a consolation prize in the eyes of the Piers Morgan breed of modern fan.

Fortunately, we made the *Essential FA Cup Final* back in 1997 before that all changed. Of our entire list of dozens of would-be interviewees, only the pantomime villain of the 1980 final, Willie Young (understandably enough), didn't want to relive his experiences on camera. Even those who lost famous finals spoke with fervour about their experiences: Brighton's Gordon Smith – 'And Smith must score' – spoke superbly about his infamous last-minute chance from 1983, and so too did Allan Clarke and Peter Lorimer of Leeds as they recalled their 1970 replay defeat to Chelsea. Their undiminished dislike of the King's Road fancy dans intercut perfectly with the twinkly Chelsea interviewees David Webb and Peter Osgood and some of the most brutal tackling in football history. Neither referee Eric Jennings nor gentleman commentator Kenneth Wolstenholme could quite compute the thuggery they were witnessing, and somehow 22 men remained on the pitch throughout both games. It was no exaggeration to say that by 1997 the Old Trafford replay would have been a five-a-side game by half-time. It made for a great sequence, though.

Yet again it was the old-timers who were the most memorable. We were lucky enough to track down a couple of pre-war winners. Bert Barlow told us about playing in Portsmouth's 1939 side. Having recorded one of the biggest shocks in FA Cup Final history – a 4-1 victory over mighty Wolves – the celebrations ended with Bert waking up next morning, dimly remembering having brought the trophy home, then turning the house upside down looking for it with his wife, before finally locating it under the bed. Even longer ago, George Mutch had played for Preston North End against Huddersfield in the 1938 final, which had been the first to be televised live by the BBC. We tracked George down – he was by now a sprightly 85-year-old living in sheltered accommodation in Aberdeen, and we drove up there one afternoon from Glasgow having just interviewed Gordon Smith.

By all accounts, that 1938 game was awful. It was goalless at 90 minutes, and deep into extra time commentator Tommy Woodroffe became a 'You'll win nothing with kids'-style hostage to fortune when he said on the air, 'If there's a goal now, I'll eat my hat.' In the 119th minute, though, the young Mutch was brought down in the penalty area. As he described it to us, he'd been hurt in the collision, but by the time he'd been treated by the trainer, his team-mates (Bill Shankly included) had disappeared into the distance. George was left with no option but to take the spot kick himself. Judging by the newsreel footage, he closed his eyes, parted the keeper's hair with an almighty hoof and the ball crashed into the net off the crossbar. And Tommy Woodroffe subsequently ate a straw hat.[18]

---

18 The hat incident was still not Tommy's most notorious broadcast. Trawl YouTube for his 'refreshed' 1937 live radio commentary on the Spithead royal naval review of 1937. Or Google 'The fleet's lit up'. You won't be disappointed. 'Listing to starboard' would be a polite nautical description.

The *Essential FA Cup Final* weighed in, appropriately enough, at just over 90 minutes, and featured everyone from Sir Tom Finney to Ricky Villa, some marvellous archive sequences and links (including a gratuitous scene in the Wembley bath) from FA Cup winners Lineker and Hansen. It was transmitted the evening before the last of a continuous sequence of 54 live BBC FA Cup Finals. I went to this one – the one and only time Middlesbrough have reached the final, and they promptly went behind to Roberto Di Matteo's screamer for Chelsea after 43 seconds and lost. Of course they did. Di Matteo's goal went in off the middle of the same crossbar – or at least a crossbar at the same end of Wembley – as George Mutch's penalty 59 years earlier, come to think of it.

With an elevation to assistant editor following in 1998, that magnum opus was the last documentary I produced, although I was still able regularly to commission others to trawl those wonderful BBC archives and make creative pieces – the television equivalent of becoming a grandparent. I never again helped get a music great to produce a theme tune like I had Ray Davies, though I did lend my support to Ian Finch's inspired, and ultimately successful, mission to persuade Stevie Wonder to allow us to make our 2014 World Cup titles to his glorious 'Another Star'. There is a happy crossover between sport and music – many top exponents of one have a huge admiration for the other and see it as an escape from their own sphere – so there were other fleeting rock star encounters over the years.

I don't count passing Debbie Harry in the corridor at Television Centre, somehow getting it into my head that she was someone I knew whose name I'd forgotten, and blurting out, 'Hi there, how are you?' She smiled and said, 'I'm fine, thanks. How are you?' just as I realised who she was, which was very generous of her. I met another favourite of mine, Roddy Frame of Aztec Camera – an oasis of guitar-playing and fine songwriting in a desert of mid-80s synthesiser pap – backstage after a gig at Shepherd's Bush Empire, courtesy of Roddy's friend Roger Black. Then I had half an hour's chat with a genuine global star, Robert Plant, when he came over to talk to Mark Lawrenson (who I happened to be standing next to) at Adrian Chiles's leaving do, in a W12 wine bar after the latter parted company with *The One Show*. The Wolves fan and Led Zeppelin rock god had just appeared on Adrian's final programme for a spot of Black Country bantz with the long-suffering Baggie. He was almost absurdly down to earth and mostly wanted to talk about football, rather than music. The same thing happened when Robbie Williams (him again) turned up and spent a Saturday afternoon on the sofa in the *MOTD* production office when he was rehearsing for *Strictly*. Our TV Centre production office backed on to a corridor of dressing rooms, so we'd get Len Goodman putting his head round the door asking how West Ham were getting on, or Roger Lloyd-Pack (Trigger from *Only Fools and Horses*) watching a Spurs game with us between rehearsals. The only time I ever had my photo taken in the workplace was when Mary McCartney, daughter of Sir Paul, but a fine artist in her own right, was invited in by Gary to take some behind-the-scenes photos for a Macmillan Cancer Charity project based on back-up teams.

One final music-related story. Shortly before Gary Lineker's wedding to Danielle in 2009, he hosted a stag dinner for some BBC Sport colleagues and other friends in a dining room above a club in Soho. After our meal, we headed downstairs for a drink in the piano bar. A pianist was playing Gershwin, Cole Porter and the like and was in due course joined by a young woman who'd left the bar to sing along to a couple of old standards. Rather well, as it happened. 'Every Time We Say Goodbye' by Ella Fitzgerald was duly struck up, and all was going smoothly until the singer slightly lost track of the words to the second verse. I grew up with American Songbook classics playing in our house, so decided to go over and prompt her sotto voce with the first couple of words of the next line or two. This went well, and after deserved applause for her performance, I had a chat with this would-be diva. 'You're pretty good,' I said. 'Ever thought of doing this for a living?' I then wandered back to my seat next to Andrew Clement. 'She's good,' I reiterated and then, looking across at her again, 'She even looks a bit like Lily Allen.' 'That's because she is Lily Allen, you prat,' was Andrew's succinct reply.

We had two more surreal off-duty moments during the 2006 World Cup. First, Frank Skinner and David Baddiel walked into a karaoke session in a bar one evening, just as our stats team were launching into their 'Three Lions', a song which had been a big hit in Germany after Euro '96.[19] They joined in, to raucous approval. Secondly, there was our wrap party in another bar in Berlin when Noel Gallagher came in through one door just as the great American film director Spike Lee walked through another with the actor Clive Owen. Noel had been interviewed by the BBC before the final across town at the Olympic Stadium and had asked our producer if anything was arranged for later. He was at a loose end and fancied talking football into the night over a beer with Lineker, Hansen and co. Clive Owen had come into our studio earlier in the tournament through a mutual friend of Niall Sloane, and had then invited Spike, in whose movie *Inside Man* he'd recently starred, to our post-World Cup Final drink. Spike was a friend of Thierry Henry's and was wearing a French shirt with 'Henry 12' sewn on its back as he drowned his sorrows after his mate's team's defeat on penalties.

Other than *Sports Personality of the Year*, especially in 1999 when Muhammad Ali collected a 'Sports Personality of the Millennium' award and quietly told David Beckham 'You're pretty', that was probably the starriest BBC-led gathering I ever encountered. On second thoughts, it might have been held at bay by the leaving do of one of the greatest characters I've ever had the privilege to have known. Chris Lewis had once had trials as a goalkeeper at the club he supports, Norwich City, he's a musician (he was once in a band with Ian McLagan of the Small Faces and later wrote the

---

19 Germany's victorious homecoming celebrations featured Klinsmann and co sardonically bellowing 'Football's Coming Home' outside Frankfurt town hall.

BBC TV boxing theme 'Sir Percy'), he was a light entertainment and sport floor manager, then, for the last three decades or so, a boxing, football and equestrian event outside broadcast director. As a freelance producer, he directed the equestrian events in Greenwich for the IOC's host broadcaster at the 2012 Olympics. As a man about town in the 70s and 80s, he variously floor managed the Miss World show for a number of years, shared a flat with Dennis Waterman, double-dated two of Pan's People with *Jesus of Nazareth* star Robert Powell and had Les Dawson to stay in his spare room whenever *Blankety Blank* was recording at Television Centre. His contacts and joke books were equally voluminous – sample deadpan joke: 'Terrible news. Our local librarian died. We had to hold a minute's noise.' When Chris bowed out from the BBC in 2006, Jesus of Nazareth, other actor friends like Warren Clarke and virtually every living BBC Sport presenter and commentator were present.

The crowning glory for Chris's guests was to be met and greeted as we arrived at the door of The Boathouse pub in Putney by one of the greatest boxers of all time. Marvin Hagler had flown in from Milan specially, and simply wanted to shake hands with every one of Chris's friends. I'm only scratching the surface here: if Chris ever writes a book it will contain some of the greatest showbiz and sport stories you've ever read.

Occasionally, an exciting crossover between sport and television involved an injection of comedy. When I edited my first live FA Cup Final build-up in 2002 after the contract had returned, *The Office* was one series old and a cult hit on BBC Two. We commissioned Ricky Gervais to write and perform a David Brent monologue of inept motivational gobbledegook aimed at finalists Arsenal and Chelsea. My colleague Steve Boulton had a comedy production background and produced it. Sample line to David Seaman: 'Of course moustaches are still fashionable. In the North.'

Gary Lineker and I had a shared enthusiasm for *Monty Python's Life of Brian,* and occasionally shoehorned references into our scripts; for example, Kevin Keegan's less successful second spell in charge at Newcastle was described as 'He's not the Messiah, he's a very naughty boy.' Michael Palin, on a visit to Salford, agreed to record his score predictions for us to challenge Lawro's for the weekly *Football Focus* segment. Ahead of Palin's visit, I'd been banging on in the office about the post-Python episode of *Ripping Yarns* in which he'd played an old-time supporter of the perennially useless Barnstoneworth United, who smashed up his home every Saturday after yet another thumping for his team. By this time – 2013 – the production team had mostly been born in the 80s or even 90s, so had no idea what I was talking about. I lamented this fact to Michael when he arrived, and he duly slipped in, as his score prediction for West Brom v Arsenal, 'Eight-bloody-one', the line his *Ripping Yarns* character had howled just before he threw the mantelpiece clock through his front room window. The clip was duly dug out of the vaults and made the air after all. What a pro.

As well as the chance to meet, and work with extraordinary talents from different fields, the job sometimes gave us opportunities to travel to some remarkable places. My favourite work excursions often involved places I'd probably never have visited otherwise. I've been to almost all corners of the British Isles with the BBC and have mentioned Japan, Korea, Donetsk, northern Finland and Split as unusual overseas trips. I also combined working with Martin Webster's team at the Bislett Games athletics in Oslo with a midsummer side trip (paid for out of my own pocket, of course) to the Arctic Circle afterwards.

In 2001, shortly after we'd regained the England contract, Carl from Widnes, Andrew and I were asked to help fill an FA sponsors' plane, hotel and ticket allocation for an Albania v England World Cup qualifier in Tirana. This had been undersubscribed by the corporate types who seemingly preferred more glamorous jollies, but I was in my element. An Islamic culture in Europe, coupled with gargantuan Stalinist monuments, and Norman Wisdom as the stadium's half-time entertainment[20], running around the pitch and performing his trademark pratfalls to rapturous applause. What more could you want? That trip, free though it was, almost certainly wouldn't be allowed by the BBC bosses, or even offered, in the modern era, but it was a fascinating experience. Sven's England won 3-1 with Andrew Cole scoring his only goal in an England shirt. Other than a brick bouncing off the coach window right next to me and Clare Tomlinson, Sky's then England reporter, as we left the stadium, it was a joy from start to finish.

Most of the overseas travel I did with BBC Sport was to other European countries. The Atlanta Olympics and the 2002, 2010 and 2014 World Cups were major exceptions. As were two other contrasting trips to Africa. In our search for live football, and with African stars like Emmanuel Adebayor and Didier Drogba becoming increasingly prominent in our Premier League, the BBC secured the contract for a string of the biennial African Cups of Nations in the early part of the 21st century. The BBC as a whole often accompanied these tournaments with seasons of Africa-related programming, and, budgets permitting, we put a lot of effort into sending commentators and reporters to the host countries, recruiting African guests like Nigeria's former captain Stephen Keshi and showcasing the cultures and stories beyond the football. With the tournaments taking place in the European winter, so clashing with our domestic football output, I was never able to make it to any of them. The closest I came was a three-day visit to Accra, Ghana with Niall Sloane in 2007 to represent the BBC at the draw for the following January's tournament, then work out what our schedule of live games would be and what facilities we'd need.

This became a memorable trip for two reasons. Firstly, the draw itself. That was about as far removed from the dull British 'the first voice you will hear' approach as it's possible to imagine. We

---

20 Norman Wisdom's films were the only Western entertainment allowed in Albania under the repressive four-decade Communist regime of Enver Hoxha. Hoxha saw Wisdom as a symbol of the underdog worker subverting capitalism, as represented by his on-screen boss Mr Grimsdale.

arrived at the venue to find a row going on in the foyer because delegates arriving to attend an international economics forum were being asked to leave. The venue had been double-booked, and football was naturally deemed more important than finance. There were fire-dancers (slightly alarmingly in what appeared to be an all-wooden auditorium), wildly exuberant musical acts and the bizarre spectacle of the tournament's mascot, a man dressed up as a multi-coloured chicken. Despite having invited Abedi Pele, George Weah and other African greats to draw the balls out of the pots, the organisers found they were one short, so the chicken was summoned to help. Sadly, his mascot outfit included huge rubbery red claws too big for the pots, so he had to remove these and use his human hands to complete the draw. If this ever happened to Ted Croker and friends in the committee room at the Football Association in Lancaster Gate, Bryon Butler never told us about it.

Then there was Marcel Desailly. Marcel had worked for us as a pundit at the previous year's World Cup in Berlin and as a reporter at previous African Cups of Nations – everyone in African and European football knew him, so access was never a problem. Marcel was born in Ghana and subsequently moved to France with his mother, siblings and stepfather, who was a French consul in Accra. Having also lived and worked for a number of years in Milan and London, Marcel's very much a citizen of the world, and while still mostly based in France, he'd had a house built in the outskirts of the Ghanaian capital and was staying there this particular weekend. The draw had taken place on the Friday, and Marcel had invited Niall and me for lunch the next day. A long drive out of the city and we finally drew up outside a gated community. We were ushered inside to be greeted by the spectacle of Marcel and one of his cousins racing quad bikes around the lawn. He took us inside and began to switch on several televisions all showing different European football matches – some live, since Accra is on the Greenwich meridian and it was Saturday. Then mountains of chicken in peanut sauce, rice and all manner of exotic vegetables arrived courtesy of Marcel's live-in housekeeper/cook and we sat down to a gargantuan feast.

It was only then that Niall and I clocked the chairs around the dining table – many were upholstered in various shades of blue fabric with non-matching trim, a couple were white and at least one was covered in red and black stripes. On closer inspection there were badges, manufacturers' crests and, in some cases, sponsors' logos on them. To Marcel's amusement, Niall and I went around the table piecing this together. One of the blue ones had an 8 on the front and a France '98 logo, there were two from 2000 – the Euros and a Chelsea FA Cup Final inscription. Red and black stripes represented the rossoneri of Milan. OK, so the white one with light blue trim must be Marseille, but what about the other white one, this time with red trim? Ah, yes, when Milan battered Barcelona 4-0 in that Champions League Final in Athens and you scored a brilliant fourth goal yourself, you were wearing your change kit. Marcel, entirely logically, saw little point in storing away the shirts in which he'd won so many trophies, so had put them to practical use, setting visitors a football trivia test which the BBC duo eventually passed with flying colours.

The other trip I made to Africa, also in 2007, was unforgettable for different reasons. Steve Boulton and I, editors of *Football Focus* and *Match of the Day* respectively, had always done whatever was asked of us when Comic Relief and Sport Relief came calling. I was never a big fan of David Cameron as prime minister – especially after his 'delicious BBC cuts' line when the licence fee freeze led to job losses – but I did support his pledge to ring-fence the UK's overseas aid budget. Beyond that, the national broadcaster putting aside one entertaining evening a year to raise tens of millions of pounds and show viewers extraordinary projects they've helped to fund, both in the UK and in some of the poorest countries on the planet, seems fair enough to me. BBC Sport, by definition, was and remains right at the heart of Sport Relief but we also helped where we could with Comic Relief. Clearly, those who've donated want to be sure their money is well spent – all the more so after some of the recent scandals involving Oxfam and other charities – and the process of inviting donations from the public, then showing them films of funded projects on the ground, was a transparent, and often moving, way of assuaging any doubts.

I only met one person during my time at BBC Sport who expressed reservations about any of this, echoing ex-BBC Radio 4 *Today* programme editor Rod Liddle and his 'Raising money for a continent of despots – now that's funny' article of 2017 in the *Sunday Times*. The money raised all goes straight to projects not national governments, why let the facts get in the way of a spot of dog-whistling, eh? Liddle had previously trashed our African Cup of Nations coverage in 2004 when tiny and recently war-torn Rwanda had qualified. To many of us, this was a remarkable human-interest story but Rod, writing in *The Times*, took the following shock-jock angle: 'the Hutus and Tutsis seemed quite adept at genocide whereas they're absolutely shite at football'.

In 2007, someone senior in BBC Sport expressed Liddle-lite sentiments when told that *Football Focus* editor Steve Boulton and I had been invited, along with some of the football talent, to visit and film some of the Sport Relief-funded projects in Uganda. I was subjected to a tirade about how Africa was a basket case, he'd never go anywhere near the disease-ridden place and couldn't see why we'd want to do so, and, moreover, the BBC shouldn't be involved in any of this stuff anyway. Lovely. And people think the corporation is overrun by PC-obsessed, bleeding-heart liberals.

Undeterred, Steve Boulton, a couple of Comic Relief people and I flew to Kampala (or more specifically, the infamous Entebbe airport) accompanied by Les Ferdinand, 5 Live's Mark Pougatch and Roger Johnson, then of BBC South Sport, who was to gather material for the BBC regions. In a country that had been slowly recovering from the economic and social chaos inflicted by Idi Amin's monstrous regime of the 70s, we visited everything from harrowing AIDS-related projects to uplifting co-operative farms and schemes to recycle rubbish and turn it into artwork. Les Ferdinand bonded immediately with everyone he met in a country obsessed with the Premier League (though he was seemingly feted as much for being related to Rio as for his own achievements) and gave speeches to enraptured school assemblies about lifestyle choices, especially the need to practise safe sex. This was particularly important in a country cursed by the HIV/AIDS epidemic (we met some of those who'd been affected) and into which US Christian evangelists were pouring money to mount an alternative, and unrealistic, pro-chastity campaign.

Although we witnessed some extremes, the like of which I'd never seen, the trip reminded us all of the greatness of which humanity is capable, especially when given a gentle helping hand. On our final day we visited Kisenyi, the biggest shanty town in Kampala. Here, alongside improvements in sanitation and health care, Sport Relief had helped to fund the construction of a netball court. The local girls had rallied behind this to such an extent that their team was now a force to be reckoned with in the Ugandan national league, taking on all comers, including the middle-class kids from the few private schools. As the sun set, hundreds of people gathered on the court to dance and sing beautiful harmonic music and play drums and other instruments. I don't think any of us will ever forget the experience, or – in my case, at least – ever feel quite so humble, and lucky, again.

Perhaps the most unforgettable sporting event I ever worked on came relatively late in my career, much closer to home, but still way outside my comfort zone. Once I was promoted permanently to editor, I'd worked almost entirely on football programmes. However, the 2012 Olympics in London was being held in the close season and with many senior people having left the BBC ahead of the move to Salford the previous year, Dave Gordon, the BBC's head of major events, a Fulham fan with whom I'd always got on well, asked me to take charge of the second live gallery on the daytime shift. The first gallery would be staffed by our most experienced all-round sports editors – Carl from Widnes and Ron Chakraborty were two of them. They'd look after the BBC One output, so nearly all the live athletics, swimming and cycling would be shown on their watch. As a guest editor, working alongside ace football studio director Kelly Faulkner, I'd be navigating an alternative offering on BBC Three, and an all-embracing red button and online offering would sweep up everything else. We'd even been given a familiar football face to front our shows in Manish Bhasin.

It all sounded daunting, but Dave is the single greatest planner I've ever met and had the whole 17 days mapped out on the most complex spreadsheets known to mankind. I took some pride in swotting up on it all as though I was about to sit my 'A' levels again, to such an extent that Dave was amused to overhear me on the phone discussing the prospects for the Finn and 470 classes with the sailing commentators as though I'd heard of either a few weeks earlier. And if the viewing public didn't like what the network editors were doing, we were no longer making *Grandstand*, so they could bypass us and find their favourite sport on the red button or website.

I'm loath to say how much I enjoyed London 2012, because I know the loss of key personnel around the Salford move and a tight budget meant some of the VT team in particular were horribly stretched, working extreme hours and staying in ropey accommodation. Many were just glad to emerge at the other end in one piece. I have to say that, by contrast, the Liverpool Street Travelodge was passable, the burrito stall at the IBC was pretty good and, professionally, I had an absolute ball from the moment Danny Boyle's phenomenal opening ceremony showed the world that this was going to be something special.

With so much happening simultaneously, even the supposed second-choice sports on our show produced live British gold medals (in canoe slalom and team showjumping) and we bounced around from sport to sport for hours on end every day with almost no hiccups. I set us the challenge of showing a little of every sport at some point across the 17 days – from memory, a Greco-Roman wrestling medal bout completed the set – and I also made a point of transmitting every feature and montage anyone had made which hadn't gone out anywhere else.

London 2012 also presented the chance to work with many people I'd admired from afar while working on football. I knew Clare Balding a little, but her role (one of the many she had across the Games) at the equestrian events at Greenwich meant I engaged directly with her professionally for the first time. I tested her ability to extemporise while we were waiting for the GB showjumping team, now Olympic champions, to appear for their triumphant interview, but Clare nonchalantly staged a five-minute royal walkabout during which she chatted merrily to anyone she could find in the jubilant crowd, then brought in Nick Skelton and team. Ore Oduba, Jonathan Edwards and Matt Baker were a pleasure to deal with at the boxing, canoeing and gymnastics respectively, and the latter sport saw a former Olympian join Kelly and me to help us through one immensely complicated afternoon.

I'd last shared a gallery with our head of sport, Barbara Slater, at the Preston Guildhall in 1994 when I'd been the editor and she'd been the transmission director of the World Indoor Bowls Championships. She'd inherited sporting genes from her father Bill of Wolves and England football fame and was remarkably good at bowls when we tried it in Preston. I've also chatted to Barbara about midnight feasts with Nadia Comaneci and once saw her walk across a room on her hands when challenged to prove that she could still do it. I don't suppose Barbara does that these days in front of the BBC Board of Governors or when she's negotiating with the IOC, but she was thrilled beyond measure when the British men won their first team gymnastics medal in a century[21]. I was pleased, too, but mostly relieved that Kelly and she

---

21 Along with 'Team GB', I refuse to use the modern term 'medalling'. Its only acceptable use was with a different spelling when a captured *Scooby Doo* villain railed against Shaggy and the kids.

had managed – with minimal help from me – to ensure that we cut between the individual apparatus feeds at the right time and turned the rest around on videotape so that all the right routines made the air.

In an echo of my first Olympics in Barcelona 20 years earlier, working on the day shift meant I could spend most evenings watching the events. With the exception of the swimming and gymnastics events – small arenas and intense interest from the American broadcaster NBC made those the hottest media tickets in town – the accreditation which got us into the International Broadcast Centre mostly got us into the venues, too. Astonishingly, this included the stadium during the athletics. Despite the US's impressive track record in the sprints in particular, the NBC contingent – there were hundreds of them, with their own inner sanctum in the IBC, complete with extra security checks – were far from mob-handed at the Olympic sport we consider supreme, but which they call track and field and largely ignore. The fact that the great Michael Johnson works as a BBC pundit tells its own story. Thanks to floor manager Nick Bushell rustling up a spare commentary box pass, I saw Michael Phelps win one of his record 23 swimming golds, but a whole gang of us were able to be at Super Saturday when Jess Ennis, Greg Rutherford and Mo Farah all struck gold within an hour of each other.

For one magical fortnight, we seemed to blossom as a nation as we welcomed the world to London. I have an abiding memory of heading out of the Olympic Park towards Stratford Tube station late one evening. One of the army of volunteers – a young lad of maybe 18 – was sitting on top of what appeared to be a tennis umpire's chair. As the crowds passed by, if he spotted anyone in national colours – be they Japanese or Finnish – he had a stab at saying 'Thank you' and 'goodbye' in their language from a list he'd printed out. That sort of cosmopolitan behaviour might see him branded a 'citizen of nowhere' these few short years later, but it'll come back into fashion one day.

So that's more or less it for my BBC Sport career. As it transpired, I had one more football tournament left in me, and a marvellous swansong at that: the 2014 World Cup in Brazil. We had a World Cup rookie in our Rio studio – Robbie Savage. To be fair to Robbie, he's a bit of a knowing self-parody, but he's good-natured and the presenters and ex-pros all like him, and he'll cheerfully admit that he wasn't the greatest player ever to grace the Premier League. This regular gambit backfired slightly when he tried to tell Thierry Henry on air in Rio that underdogs could match a better team through sheer work-rate and cited his Leicester team of journeymen as an example, who (he claimed) had often troubled Thierry's Arsenal aristocrats. Thierry thought about this assertion, adjusted his collar slightly and drily muttered the unanswerable put-down, 'We managed.'

Robbie was the first footballer I'd worked with who was openly fascinated and impressed by fast cars and designer clothes. He duly decided that Andrew Clement and I, as senior BBC figures, were far too scruffy and should buy some 'new gear'. The fact that two resolutely unstylish men in their 50s might not want to emulate Robbie's distinctive image may not have occurred to him. Matters reached a head in the hotel one morning at breakfast. I was tired, my ears were playing up and I'd already snapped at Robbie the previous day for being amused/amazed by my reading a book on my morning off. I came down in my usual non-designer polo shirt and a pair of beige shorts. It wasn't yet 9am, but Robbie was already in full Tigger mode, bouncing around the buffet. 'How much did them [sic] shorts cost, Armo?' he asked. I was about to grunt back that I had no idea and didn't care when I noticed that Robbie himself was sporting undoubtedly expensive, but nonetheless garish, fluorescent orange shorts. 'I'd have a go back,' I said, 'if I could work out where your shorts end and the fake tan starts.' Philip Neville, a veteran of a feisty Old Trafford dressing room, gave this retort a round of applause and Robbie hooted with laughter, acknowledging some #topbantz.

I continued to edit *Match of the Day* fairly regularly, but with escalating ear problems, I began to move increasingly towards desk duties – temporarily I hoped, though sadly that wasn't to be. I became the BBC person in charge of (exec'ing in telly speak) the plethora of sport productions now made by independent companies. Successive governments had tried to open up the alleged monolith of the BBC to competition by insisting that a fixed percentage of programmes had to be made by production teams from outside the corporation.

This quota system meant that in my later years snooker, darts and bowls were put out to tender and made up the bulk of the required programme hours. Football League highlights and some of our women's football productions were also produced outside BBC Sport at various times. This entailed a good deal of rather tedious administration and frequent editorial policy consultations, but also some more pleasant tasks like visits to the Crucible to see Hazel Irvine, Jason Mohammad, a fine IMG production team and an illustrious group of snooker pundits. Then there were the sticky carpets and unique atmosphere of BDO darts at Frimley Green with Colin Murray and Bobby George, and Great Yarmouth in January with Rishi Persad and his adoring fan club of bowls-loving pensioners.

I limped on for a while longer, but my final programme as editor – though I didn't know it at the time – came on Boxing Day 2014. I edited *Final Score* and slipped one final iffy script line through Jason Mohammad's defences: 'Back out of the house after the Christmas break, by popular demand – not least from his family – Robbie Savage.'

9.

'What happens next?'

… as David Coleman used to say, linking into a clip on *A Question of Sport*, the videotape freezing tantalisingly just before some sporting oddity took place.

Well, we moved back to London in 2016, and with Boro back in the Premier League for the first time in eight years, and my Saturdays now free, I bought a Riverside season ticket next to my Uncle Michael and Auntie Christine from Bishop Auckland and gave Virgin Trains most of my redundancy money in fortnightly instalments. Other than a double over Sunderland, which barely counts, Boro won three games all season. Including the three goals against Sunderland, our feeble final tally was 27 in 38 matches, so two fewer than Harry Kane managed on his own that season. On our travels, we handed champions Leicester a 94th-minute penalty equaliser after a rare decent performance and were early guinea pigs at the initially police-free new West Ham home venue – the worst view and nastiest atmosphere I've encountered since the 1980s. Then there was Brad Guzan's wobbly goalkeeping[22] and the one and only time my long-standing fellow Boro watcher Rob

---

22 The hapless Brad was nutmegged for all three goals as Boro's relegation was confirmed at Chelsea, prompting this memorable social media exchange: 'I wish Brad Guzan would close his legs.' Reply: 'I wish his mother had closed her legs.'

Skilbeck and I have ever booed one of our players, when a flouncing Gaston Ramirez took his ball home one long afternoon at Stoke.

Enough, already. I won't bore you with my problems. Let's concentrate on some thoughts about what the future might hold for the sport we love and for the wider world of broadcasting. I've watched football for almost 50 years and have worked on it for more than half that time. Consequently, I have a great deal of sympathy with our beloved England manager Gareth Southgate when he once said, 'I love the game but hate the industry.'

A low point for me came when I worked alongside BBC News in 2010 on live coverage of the announcement of the host nations for FIFA's 2018 and 2022 World Cups. We knew international football governance had been shoddy for some time, but this was still a real eye-opener. Gary Lineker was in Zurich along with Prince William, David Cameron and others lobbying for England to host in 2018, and I kept in touch with him by text. With the announcement a few minutes away, I relayed news from Gary that, despite numerous earlier face-to-face promises, England had garnered precisely two votes from the world's football federations so had been eliminated after the first ballot. Russia had merit as the venue chosen for 2018, Qatar perhaps less so for 2022, but all manner of murk has subsequently been dredged up about the selection process. FIFA and UEFA do now appear to be cleaning up their acts since Sepp Blatter, Michel Platini and others have departed; Gary agreed to host the draw for Russia 2018 after lengthy discussions with FIFA's new deputy secretary general, and ex-AC Milan and Croatia star, Zvonimir Boban, during which he was persuaded that they're trying to put their house in order.

Another area in which progress is being made – albeit falteringly – is technology. Blatter and his cohorts had for years vetoed any attempts to use video replays to help officials, leaving the world's biggest and richest sport decades behind rugby, cricket and tennis, to name but three. FIFA got lucky twice at the 2010 World Cup: firstly, Frank Lampard's 'over-the-line' moment against Germany came in a game that England lost 4-1 anyway; and referee Howard Webb missing Nigel De Jong's kung-fu kick on Xabi Alonso in the final could have cost Spain their first-ever World Cup trophy, but (just about) didn't[23].

As I've said, as *Match of the Day* editor, I became increasingly tired of having to devote analysis time to two or three key decisions a week which the beleaguered officials had simply got wrong. Moreover, in most of those other sports – cricket and tennis, in particular – hundreds of points or runs are scored every game, so no one decision is likely to change the outcome to the extent that a goal does in football, but still the desire to eliminate mistakes holds sway.

The 'there's no technology on a Sunday morning at Wormwood Scrubs' argument never even began to make sense to me and is heard less often these days. The slightly more plausible 'it evens itself out' line can work across a league season, but certainly doesn't apply if you're Chesterfield deprived of the only conceivable FA Cup Final appearance in their history in 1997, or even, if like Amanda and me, you've travelled for hours for a football-centred weekend in Norfolk (and a catch-up with my old college team-mate, one-time Norwich City reporter Rick Waghorn) only to have the match ruined by a nonsensical red card for Boro's centre-forward after 28 minutes. That (Rudy Gestede, February 2018) was duly rescinded the following Monday but nobody compensates the away fans for a long and wasted journey, which ought to have been rescued by technology and five seconds of an extra official's time.

Thankfully, neither that Chesterfield moment nor indeed the Geoff Hurst/Azerbaijani linesman kerfuffle will happen again at the top level, the authorities having finally agreed to sanction the gradual introduction of goal-line technology from 2012, a mere decade or so after it was eminently achievable. As for the less

---

23 FIFA still managed to ruin that 2010 World Cup as a spectacle by introducing their commercial partner Adidas's lightweight Jabulani match ball which virtually eliminated accurate long passes, crosses and shots from the tournament.

objective areas of officiating, despite the mixed success of attempts to introduce it so far, especially in the FA Cup where it's sometimes bordered on the farcical, I still believe that the VAR (video assistant referee) system will eventually prove preferable to three pairs of fallible eyes assessing a pivotal incident just the once, at full speed. Those involved just need to follow the stated objective of only 'correcting clear and obvious errors'. Where it went wrong at the 2018 World Cup were the occasions – sadly, including the penalty awarded to France in the final – when the referee or his VAR team lost sight of that. In the end, any system is only as good as those managing and operating it, and the World Cup officials varied considerably in their levels of competence. The same as it ever was, although for me, that one penalty overturned when a brave referee realised Neymar had conned him made the whole exercise worthwhile. VAR then reversing an entirely understandable, but incorrect, offside decision to allow the South Korean goal which effectively eliminated Germany should cement its future.

Maybe football should copy tennis or cricket, where each team has two or three unsuccessful appeals a set or innings. Yes, the game would stop occasionally, but not after every goal or incident: coaches would quickly learn not to use up their reviews unnecessarily. You wouldn't lose a review when you know Neymar's dived against you or when Maradona's punched the ball into your net, and it should become obvious to would-be cheats that they won't succeed. A few more cards for trying it on would help, too. And where it's marginal or unclear, as so many handballs are, stick with the referee's original decision, as they do with 'umpire's call' in cricket. There are still arguments following certain video referrals in that sport, but at least palpably incorrect decisions are now reversed. Where it's a question of in or out – run-outs, over the goal line, in the box or not, tennis calls – there's a scientific answer, not guesswork. Can you imagine a blanket finish in the Derby or Olympic 100m final being determined by one person's instantaneous best guess? OK, so John McEnroe's career would have been less colourful if he hadn't been able to rail against the officials, but surely that would have been a worthwhile price to pay for accurate decision-making?

Paradoxically, in many other areas, football has moved on in leaps and bounds since I first become a regular on the away terraces in the early 1980s, and then first worked on the sport later in the decade. The game on the pitch is the best it's ever been. The speed, overall technical ability and work rate of Pep's Manchester City or Klopp's Liverpool is breathtaking, especially when witnessed in the flesh. Just watch some old footage of the wheezing full-backs and 'hapless custodian' keepers of the black-and-white era, or even the hacking down of skilful players and endless backpasses of the 70s and 80s. Or go, as I sometimes do, to watch a decent level of non-league football. Everyone tries to play out from the back these days, attempts are made at a high press and every team has someone who can sling in a mean dead ball. When I occasionally took the 268 bus to Darlington to watch lower league football in the late 70s, the standard was agricultural by comparison. Pitches are far better now, and conducive to good football: the game's moved on, it's no longer a question of simply hoofing it up to the big man amidst scything tackles and swinging elbows as it was on that Feethams mudheap.

Off the pitch, too, the game is scarcely recognisable. When I first worked on *Sportsnight,* it was possible – I know, because I did it – to arrange an interview with the England manager ahead of a crucial World Cup qualifier with just one phone call. England needed a draw in Poland to reach Italia '90, so I rang Bobby Robson's secretary at the FA and was put through to the great man himself. We duly arranged a visit from Motty after a training session at Bisham Abbey. Admittedly, only BBC and ITV Sport would have been looking for a TV interview in those less complex times, but 20 years on it would have been easier to organise an audience with the Pope than be put through to Fabio Capello.

The same applied at club level – the demands on clubs in an era of 24-hour channels and much increased overseas interest meant that meaningful access to Premier League players became more and more difficult. There is now a wall of agents and club PR people standing between them and the viewer. Even when someone says something interesting or off-message – Roy Keane's attack on the 'prawn sandwich brigade', for example – the media feeding frenzy turns it into a 'storm' or 'rage', the corporate shutters come down, and insecure managers and agents try to prevent any repetition. Top footballers are very well paid indeed, and this can lead to excesses. Some of their antics are grotesque; others, like the burnt-out bathroom in a Cheshire mansion I passed every day as I drove into Salford, are just slightly childish. Mario Balotelli had some friends to stay, was bored and set off some indoor fireworks. We all did silly things when we were young, though perhaps not that.

While I understand that footballers' salaries create a gulf between the average fan and the players he or she watches, I don't see it as entirely, or even largely, the fault of top footballers. In a world of supply and demand, film stars and best-selling musicians earn equally ludicrous money. Many footballers set up foundations or, like Rio Ferdinand, give a great deal back on the quiet to the communities they come from – Peckham for Rio, or the Grenfell Tower fund in Raheem Sterling's case. Even if they don't, would anyone really want to return to the 50s when Tom Finney, one of the country's finest footballers, earned the maximum wage (£15 a week in 1953, reduced to £13 in summer, at a time when the average national wage was £10) so still worked as a part-time plumber? Clubs and their owners pocketed almost all the gate receipts during that era of the highest-ever league crowds.

I once had the honour of sitting next to Wilf Mannion – the greatest of all Middlesbrough players according to both my Granddad and my father-in-law – at a dinner in the late 90s. Wilf had been a regular in a Boro team that finished fourth in the league (they've never finished in as high a position again) when war broke out in 1939. What would have been the peak of his playing career was instead spent serving his country with the Green Howards regiment. The great Yorkshire and England cricketer Hedley Verity was killed serving alongside Wilf, along with half their company, during the Allied invasion of Sicily. Wilf played with renewed vigour for Boro after the war – my father-in-law was there in 1947 when Wilf decided to put on a show for his bride-to-be Bernadette, who was attending her first-ever football match. Visitors Blackpool lined up to applaud him off the pitch after a 4-0 Ayresome Park win, forever known locally as the Mannion Match.

It was against this backdrop, also in 1947, that Wilf was selected by the English FA for the Great Britain representative side to face the Rest of Europe in a peacetime exhibition match at Hampden Park. 'Dear Mannion,' read the letter, as Wilf described it, 'You are required in Glasgow a week on Saturday. Please bring your boots.' A third-class return railway ticket was enclosed. The day before the match, Wilf boarded the train at Darlington station. It was packed to the rafters, so he stood in the corridor all the way to Scotland. As if that wasn't bad enough, he discovered that the FA councillors had been ensconced in the first-class dining carriage since King's Cross and were just moving on to the port and cigars.

The next day Great Britain, captained by Boro's Clark Gable-lookalike right-back, George Hardwick, won 6-1 in front of a crowd of 134,000, with Wilf scoring twice. Despite being one of England's shining lights in that golden era – a forward line of Matthews, Mortensen, Lawton, Mannion and Finney scored all of England's goals between them in a 10-0 (that's ten-nil) win in Lisbon against Portugal in 1950 – Wilf never made any real money out of football. He joined non-league Cambridge City towards the end of his career because they weren't subject to the maximum-wage restriction and he ended up doing odd jobs at ICI's factory in Wilton when my Dad worked there in the 70s. Only when Steve Gibson took over the reins at Middlesbrough was he treated properly by the club he'd served with distinction for such paltry rewards. Wilf and George

Hardwick are no longer with us, but they're immortalised in playing action as fine statues outside the Riverside, just in front of the original Ayresome Park gates. If you stand at the right angle when there's a full moon they can still be seen playing keepy-up with the celestial white ball.

So the old days weren't necessarily better if Wilf's experience is anything to go by. Modern times, however, have seen a ludicrous level of intensity and name-calling around teams and rivalries. Gary Lineker and I, and most others at BBC Sport, never bought into this. The old days were certainly more courteous. My Granddad Armstrong, who lived all his life in Cockfield, a pit village outside Bishop Auckland, would happily board the bus the villagers chartered every Saturday and watch Newcastle, Sunderland or Middlesbrough, depending on who was playing at home. He wished them all well throughout the rest of his life, as did his fellow lover of football, my mother's uncle Bob Taylor, whose twin brother John played in goal for Bishop Auckland at Wembley in one of their FA Amateur Cup triumphs. Incidentally, as Harry Pearson reminds us in his wonderful (better-than-*Fever Pitch*, if you ask me) chronicle of North East football, *The Far Corner*, Cockfield had itself reached the Amateur Cup Final in 1927, a decade which saw 22 professional footballers emerge from the village in the space of three years. My Granddad knew all of them, but like my maternal grandfather, who came from nearby West Auckland and used to claim they'd reached the World Cup Final[24], I didn't listen to him sufficiently while he was still alive.

According to official censuses, the whole population of Cockfield was never greater than the 2,693 it reached in 1921, so something extraordinary was clearly going on. Even that neutrality between the Tyne, Wear and Tees's finest professional teams

---

24 They really did – the Thomas Lipton World Cup of 1909 in which a team of miners beat Juventus 6-1 in Turin in the final. Ticer Thomas, grandfather of 70s QPR and England winger Dave, was one of them. Dennis Waterman turned this remarkable story into ITV drama *A Captain's Tale*, which was broadcast towards the end of my Granddad's life.

was admirable – I have to confess that 30 seconds after Gareth Southgate lifted the Carling Cup at Cardiff in 2004, I was one of 40,000 Teessiders lustily singing 'Have you ever seen a Geordie lift a cup?' Sorry, Granddad. Unlike some around me, though, I didn't celebrate while watching Boro win at Derby County in April 2018, when news came through that Sunderland had been relegated for the second successive season after losing at home to Burton Albion. There's a point, for me at least, at which your rivals' misfortunes are of such proportions that they're no longer funny. In any case, neither Newcastle nor Sunderland fans give a monkey's about Boro – they're much too busy disliking each other – no matter how much we wish they did.

We may think modern football is ephemeral and money-dominated, but at least all the big clubs have long histories, are rooted in their communities and employ some players who've hung around long enough to be synonymous with them. There won't be an Andrés Iniesta or even a Harry Kane in the *It's a Slogout* of franchise cricket. My fear – it keeps being floated in the media – is that the biggest clubs in the Premier League will, at some point, put a stop to the collective negotiation of TV rights, which has existed since the league's inception in 1992. Far more people want to watch Manchester United versus Liverpool than Huddersfield v Burnley, especially outside the UK, the argument goes, so the individual clubs should be able to sell off their own rights.

This strikes me as a terrible idea – United and Liverpool already make far more revenue than the other two (or pretty much anyone else, for that matter) from sponsorship, global merchandising, gate receipts and regular Champions League qualification. Take away the bulk of the other clubs' TV money and you'll have an even less level playing field. La Liga, having been leant on by the Spanish government, abandoned just such a system in 2017 and returned to collective bargaining: Real Madrid and Barcelona will probably always remain far richer than the rest of the league put together – and unless someone introduces an NFL-style draft system, they'll still snap up the world's leading players – but at least the necessity of those giants having meaningful opposition to play against has been recognised.

If the mutterings grow to the extent that a big-club mutiny becomes a real threat, I hope the rest of the league, and those in any other countries affected, call their bluff, throw them all out and let them form a permanent European Super League. Without Bayern or PSG, for example, there might be a refreshing degree of doubt about who'd win the Bundesliga or Ligue 1. The need for a two-thirds majority to implement any significant change in how the Premier League is run, including the distribution of TV rights, may just keep such crass selfishness and greed at bay in English football. For the time being, at least.

Whatever happens to football and however much money calls the shots – even if you're in Scotland where the four-way battle of my youth has been reduced to a one-horse race, with any chance of a genuine competition resting on the hope that its historical rival may one day get its act together – there are still fleeting moments when the sport seems like one of the greatest forces for good on the planet. Just watch the YouTube footage of tens of thousands of Hibs fans singing at Hampden after they won the Scottish Cup in 2016 for the first time in 113 years. OK, so the Proclaimers' 'Sunshine on Leith' is a fantastic anthem to belt out in those circumstances, but if that particular rendition doesn't give you goose pimples, you're either a Hearts fan or made of stone.

Then there's the joy nearly all of football felt when Leicester City won the Premier League in 2016. I quite like Tottenham and have no particular love of Chelsea, particularly given Middlesbrough's history against them, but I jumped around the living room when Eden Hazard's equaliser for Chelsea against Spurs sealed an absolute miracle for the Foxes. Even the rather unsavoury fashion in which Ranieri's players appeared to earn him the sack the following season couldn't ruin that story. Then there's the uplifting effect football success can have on a whole nation –

Northern Ireland in 1982, Denmark in 1992, the Republic in 1994, Wales or Iceland in 2016.

To echo Gareth Southgate, the only captain to lift a major trophy for Boro in our 143-year history, even if you hate the football industry it's difficult not to love the game. I squeezed into the commentary box in the Maracana next to Jonathan Pearce at my last BBC tournament for the Colombia v Uruguay game and was left misty-eyed by James Rodriguez's breathtaking goal of the tournament; I've seen QPR come back from 4-0 down at half-time to draw 5-5 with Newcastle; I saw Fulham score four times to turn round a three-goal deficit against mighty Juventus; I've even watched Boro – 'a small town in Europe' – perform the same four-goal turnaround for the second time in three weeks to reach the 2006 UEFA Cup Final. In my mind's eye, I can still see a freeze-frame of Massimo Maccarone's 89th-minute diving header in the semi against Steaua Bucharest. Run VT, and all the Riverside aisles disappear in a sea of red, West Stand pensioners pogo like it's 1977, and grinning idiots gibber to complete strangers on the platform at Darlington station early the following morning. It doesn't matter a jot that Boro lost the final, it was an utterly beautiful experience. And the late Ali Brownlee's celebratory and lyrical local radio commentary is immortalised on the bridge outside the Riverside. 'Football – bloody hell', as someone once said.

Whatever happens with the running of the game or the ownership of clubs, every fan at every level of the game has their equivalent of Boro's Steaua or Fulham's Juve night. I think the future of the sport's safe enough: it's intrinsically pleasing to watch when it's played well and, with the possible exception of a sucker punch in boxing, there's the glorious uncertainty of knowing it's the only sport where you can play abysmally and win. I once saw Boro win 1-0 at Manchester City without having a shot on target. Sun Jihai sliced in an own goal from an innocuous cross, Robbie Fowler missed maybe 12 of City's 30 chances and the away team rode off into the sunset on Black Bess clutching a swag bag marked 'three points'. That simply can't happen in cricket or tennis, or even rugby, where that much pressure would lead to penalty kicks and a scoreline that reflected the balance of play.

Football is here to stay as the world's pre-eminent sport. Even the USA is slowly being won over, leaving the Indian sub-continent as the only major region that begs to differ. To quote a wildly romantic and impractical line from Mick Channon in our *Essential FA Cup Final* as he dreamily recalled Southampton's open-top bus trophy parade of 1976 – 'They should do away with politics and just have football.' A lovely thought, as long as Gareth Southgate, Marcel Desailly and Jürgen Klinsmann are in charge, not Sepp Blatter, Sergio Ramos and Joey Barton.

So, football's future is assured, but what of the other half of my career equation, the BBC? In true 'we're always on last' tradition, many prominent people across the political spectrum in the UK feel it's biased against them. I question aspects of the BBC's political coverage on a daily basis – one or two on-air figures appear to be untouchable and, as I've hinted previously, the preoccupation with balance has hit choppy waters in an era of fake news and self-appointed experts.

Even when 99 per cent of scientific or economic evidence points in one direction, equal airtime seemingly has to be afforded to the opposing view. In this age of social media retweets and viral posts, conspiracy theories spread like Japanese knotweed but, unless things have changed radically in the last couple of years, there is no secret loaded BBC agenda passed down from on high to thousands of employees.

In any case, any current government has a greater range of urgent preoccupations than did David Cameron and his culture secretary John Whittingdale (media heroes: Rupert Murdoch and Kelvin MacKenzie, when asked in a 2006 *Independent* Q&A) as they made menacing noises during the tenure of the coalition government. The BBC Charter isn't due for renewal until 2027: I suspect whoever's in office in the meantime is going to have more pressing issues on their plate than public-service broadcasting, as 'taking back control' continues to come home to roost.

As for the wider broadcasting landscape, I'm not sure my customary 'ask a techie' approach will suffice any more. Who could have predicted what's happened in the last ten years? I visited Chicago in May 2016 and saw the Cubs baseball team play at their magnificent 1914 ivy-clad, open-air museum, Wrigley Field. By that autumn the Cubs had reached the World Series, chasing a first success since 1908. I followed the post-season avidly from the UK on satellite TV but, as luck would have it, I was in Dortmund (having just watched Borussia's Champions League game with Sporting Lisbon) on the night of the seventh-game decider in Cleveland. It was nowhere to be found on German TV, so after trawling the internet I watched the most dramatic of overtime finales unfold using a hotel room's wi-fi on my phone, in HD, via Twitter, via something called Periscope from someone's living room TV in Chicago with echoing commentary, plus a whole family whooping and hollering. I don't think that was possible in 2008, let alone 1908. Like the Premier League live games shown in the back room of certain pubs on a Saturday afternoon, it probably wasn't technically legal either, but the whole palaver serves to illustrate just how complex and unstoppable the communications revolution has become.

The fact that I couldn't even tell you for sure where I followed the World Series in the UK that year – was it Channel 5? ESPN? BT Sport? – illustrates another problem for the modern broadcaster. The generation who felt an affinity with the BBC or ITV, or even knew for certain where and when they could find their favourite shows, is rapidly aging. The younger viewer – and even the semi-savvy 50-something – is now as likely to scan YouTube or browse Netflix as they are to watch BBC One's meticulously planned schedule in real time. You can search your digital planner for a programme name, or even actor, and never need to know on which channel it or they appear, or a transmission time. Luckily for those involved, live sport is one of the few 'appointment to view' areas of TV programming left. The roads are still quieter and the pubs packed when England play in a tournament, because people still want their joys and disappointments to be a live, and preferably shared, experience.

To return to my starting point, *Match of the Day* (and *MOTD2*) are, miraculously, still relevant to the point where viewing figures have remained constant for years against a background of fragmenting viewership for other popular genres such as soap operas. Audience sizes are never the be all and end all, as I've said previously, but if the BBC wants to continue to justify levying a licence fee, it helps to have some well-watched, sure-fire winners on its books. Even if you've been to a match, or watched one live on Sky or BT, or seen goal clips on your phone, a one-stop shop of 80 per cent action and 20 per cent analysis still works, for this viewer, at least. And millions of others – even the YouTube generation – feel the same, it seems. I hope the 'beautiful game', the BBC in general, and one of its crown jewels, *Match of the Day*, continue to survive and thrive in an uncertain world. I'll be cheering them all on.

Постсцрипт
Россия 2018

The last time I'd watched a World Cup as a member of the public, rather than working on it, was back in 1986. I was a student, my finals weren't until the following year, the time difference with Mexico meant most of the games were in the evening and I watched every game live as Gary Lineker won the Golden Boot. Four years later, Gary scored in the semi and I was in the BBC's videotape area; for the next two, he was a BBC pundit, then second presenter and I was still in VT. For the first four World Cups of the 21st century, Gary was the lead presenter and I was a programme editor babbling into his shell-like ear.

Now, it was the summer of 2018 – Gary would be the BBC's lead presenter for a fifth time. It was 32 years since I'd last watched a World Cup from an armchair. Much as that was an appetising prospect, and old and decrepit though I am, I decided, as is the fashion, to try to have my cake and eat it. I entered the FIFA ballot, secured a couple of tickets, ordered my FAN-ID, and booked flights and a hotel in Moscow.

I love international football. Not international friendlies, though – they're a bit like paying to watch Sinatra gargle. I covered dozens of them during my career, only one of which sticks in the mind – Michael Owen scoring twice in the last three minutes to secure a 3-2 win for England against Argentina in neutral Geneva in 2005. Our visit to Switzerland was also noteworthy for my being persuaded to perform the *MOTD* theme on an Alpine horn at a BBC team fondue the previous evening (15 fondues and a steak for Motty, to be more precise) and for Nancy Dell'Olio angrily rounding on Lineker and Hansen in a lounge after the match over some previous perceived slight against her 'Svennis'. Alan Hansen, never a lover of confrontation, backed away pointing at our head of football, Niall Sloane, and muttering, 'He's in charge.'

That trip apart, friendlies are generally dire – I even welcome the advent of the UEFA Nations League, which removes most of them from the calendar. The international breaks during a season need an extra injection of purpose, it's just a shame Professor Stephen Hawking is no longer around to explain how this new system works. I thought I was pretty good at understanding sporting 'what ifs': perhaps I'm out of practice, but I was all at sea a few paragraphs into the Nations League explanation proffered on UEFA's website. The good thing is that almost every international fixture will now have competitive meaning so will 'matter to someone, somewhere, presumably', to quote *Mitchell and Webb*'s masterly parody of a hyperbolic Sky Football trailer.

Perhaps it's a consequence of not supporting a Galactico club side, but international tournament football is as good as it gets as far as I'm concerned. It's pure, in that no Emirati royal or Russian oligarch can buy Kevin De Bruyne or Eden Hazard from Belgium like they can, and have, at club level. Each country is dealt a hand of cards in terms of the quality of any given generation of players and they just have to get on with it. International tournaments, especially once they reach the sudden-death stage, are sufficiently infrequent – and short and brutal enough – to be fantastically dramatic and tense.

I'm always slightly baffled by people who simply don't like sport, but every four years, when the World Cup comes around, it's hard not to feel genuine pity for them.

My previous football trip to Moscow, back in 1998, had been a bizarre experience. The BBC had lost the FA Cup and live England games a year earlier and had almost no live football to show during the regular season. The Champions League belonged to ITV, but we still held the live UEFA Cup Final rights through a European Broadcasting Union deal. It was decided to buy – on the cheap, I suspect – the first leg of the semi-final tie between Spartak Moscow and tournament favourites Inter Milan, who had the original Brazilian Ronaldo in their ranks. Jon Champion was to be the commentator and with Moscow high on my list of interesting places I'd never visited, I bagged the role of on-site producer.

It was April, so neither Jon nor I were prepared for a huge dollop of late snow, which greeted us on arrival. I'd brought a coat and a beanie hat, but my choice of footwear – normal socks and shoes – was already looking foolhardy by the time we reached our hotel. By chance, the Scottish refereeing team, led by Hugh Dallas, had been on our flight from London. Hugh had seen an iffy-looking weather forecast but reassured us that the Russians had moved the game to the home of Spartak's rivals Dynamo, because they had undersoil heating. Come matchday, I went at the crack of dawn to see Red Square and tour the Kremlin – it was wonderfully picturesque in the snow, but another footwear disaster. We headed off to the stadium in the afternoon – shoes filled with newspaper, in my case – to be greeted by one of the strangest sights I've ever witnessed at a football stadium. Upon removing the snow, the ground staff had discovered that the undersoil heating had worked far too well. All the grass on the pitch had been incinerated and we were left with a surface best described as resembling the clay of a Roland Garros tennis court with random piles of sand tipped on top of it.

We found Hugh Dallas again: he looked like a man under some pressure, presumably from UEFA with no wriggle room in the fixture calendar. It was decided that the game would have to go ahead. Inter were far from impressed when they arrived, but

Ronaldo's beach and futsal experience won the day. He scored twice as Inter returned to Italy with a 2-1 lead. They went on to win the trophy the following month, before 1998 took a decided turn for the worse for Ronaldo at the World Cup Final in Paris.

Twenty years on and once more I saw Ronaldo clinch a game in Moscow. This time, it was a Cristiano header in the Luzhniki in shorts weather as a very fortunate Portugal scraped past Morocco. I also shared some of the joy of two Senegalese fans as they beat Poland. We were surrounded by thousands of Poles, many of whom queued up to shake their hands at the final whistle. Echoes of Bobby Moore and Pele or Brett Lee and Andrew Flintoff when a glance at a still photo doesn't reveal who's won and who's lost. Vince Lombardi, the celebrated NFL coach, once said, 'Show me a good loser and I'll show you a loser.' Sorry, Vince, but to use language you'd understand, that's a crock. When do Poland and Senegal share a sentence let alone sportsmanlike comradeship, other than in sport, by the way?

Moscow as a whole was transformed just as Berlin and London were in 2006 and 2012. I stayed a few blocks behind the Bolshoi Theatre in a B&B that had been almost entirely requisitioned by Mexican fans. They took a couple of guitars out into the street one evening and soon hosted an impromptu fiesta attended by dozens of passing Peruvians, Colombians and local families. Even the couple of tough-looking Russian policemen who came to investigate the noise ended up wreathed in smiles. If only the world could be more like the World Cup.

It was an absolute joy to see England exceed expectations: a seemingly ego-free and diverse young squad and an absolute class act of a coach arguably did more for the country's morale and self-esteem in a month than the last couple of generations of politicians have in all their careers combined. Apologies to Scottish, Welsh and Northern Irish readers – especially for English politicians. Southgate's men even put the penalty shoot-out curse to bed, at least for a while.

The first World Cup I watched properly was the 1974 incarnation. I've scarcely missed a game since: Russia 2018 was undoubtedly the most consistently exciting and enjoyable of the 12 tournaments staged in that time. Drama galore, virtually no poor matches amongst the 64 played, indeed some of the greatest I've ever seen – from Spain 3 Portugal 3 on the second evening to Belgium 3 Japan 2 and France 4 Argentina 3 in the knockout phase, and Belgium's glorious first-half display in their quarter-final against Brazil. The two outstanding players in the tournament – a 19-year-old French genius and a 33-year-old Croatian maestro – spearheaded two worthy finalists. Like many other people around the world, I didn't quite know what to do with myself when it all finished.

Both UK World Cup broadcasters conveyed the spirit of an extraordinary tournament to the audiences at home. FIFA had found them both spectacular studio settings just behind the epicentre of nations mixing merrily for a month: Red Square. I popped into the broadcasters' compound one afternoon during my visit and was struck by the seamless continuity of the BBC operation. As Napoleon Bonaparte once observed, 'The graveyard is full of indispensable men.' Much as I'd like to think I made telling contributions to the coverage at previous tournaments, one glance at the BBC portacabin office told me I was as dispensable – in the nicest possible way – as any of Napoleon's generals.

Gary Lineker, Dan Walker, Andrew Clement, Phil Bigwood, Richard Hughes, Kelly Faulkner, Ian Finch and many more were working away, just carrying on where they'd left off in Rio, putting in the groundwork for many of the same on-screen faces and an excellent array of new pundits in Frank Lampard, Cesc Fabregas, Didier Drogba and Pablo Zabaleta. Even outside in the compound, most ITV people I ran into had BBC connections: I had a warm bearhug with Ian Wright, a chat with Mark Pougatch and said hello to numerous production and technical people from both the BBC and ITV. Once I was back in the UK, I watched the final on the BBC (of course) but I watched every other game perfectly happily on whichever channel was showing it. My old Moscow comrade Jon Champion accompanied by Ally McCoist – a BBC 1998 pairing, revived 20 years on by ITV – were particularly good commentary company through many a group game. If you've travelled during football tournaments, or even watched club coverage abroad, you'll know that the British audience is exceptionally well served by all its football broadcasters.

One final question I'm often asked about BBC football and *MOTD*, especially by ex-colleagues who still work on the show, is: 'Do you miss it?' I have to be honest and say no. I loved almost every moment I was involved, but hundreds and hundreds of Saturday evenings acting as the curator of a broadcasting institution are more than enough for anyone. Especially now, with my dodgy ears.

Millions watch your work live, the duration has to fit the schedules to the exact second, other than the links it's all unscripted, and there are considerable pressures (often self-inflicted) in hoping never to miss a story and to maintain balance and fairness. As the editor, you were expected to appear calm while keeping all the plates spinning. I never took any of it for granted or went through the motions, nor did the adrenaline (and excess confectionery and coffee) ever allow me to get to sleep afterwards before at least 3am.

So, no, I don't miss it, but by the same token I never miss it. A single *Match of the Day*, that is. Saturday night, or at a pinch Sunday morning, still isn't complete without it.

Index

220

INDEX